WITHDRAWN

INTERNATIONAL
SECURITY

INTERNATIONAL SECURITY

The American Rôle in Collective Action for Peace

BY

PHILIP C. JESSUP

ASSOCIATE PROFESSOR OF INTERNATIONAL LAW
IN COLUMBIA UNIVERSITY

COUNCIL ON FOREIGN RELATIONS, INC.

45 EAST 65TH STREET, NEW YORK

54108

PUBLICATIONS OF THE
COUNCIL ON FOREIGN RELATIONS

FOREIGN AFFAIRS, an American Quarterly Review, edited by Hamilton Fish Armstrong. *$5.00 a year.*

SURVEY OF AMERICAN FOREIGN RELATIONS, prepared under the direction of Charles P. Howland. Volumes for 1928, 1929, 1930 and 1931. *$5.00.*

THE UNITED STATES IN WORLD AFFAIRS (*annual*). An account of American Foreign Relations prepared by Walter Lippmann with the assistance of the research staff of the Council on Foreign Relations. Volumes for 1931, 1932 and 1933. *$3.00.*

POLITICAL HANDBOOK OF THE WORLD (*annual*), edited by Walter H. Mallory. *$2.50.*

FOREIGN AFFAIRS BIBLIOGRAPHY, 1919–1932, by William L. Langer and Hamilton Fish Armstrong. *$5.00.*

THE FOREIGN POLICY OF THE POWERS, by Jules Cambon, Richard von Kühlmann, Sir Austen Chamberlain, Dino Grandi, Viscount Ishii, Karl Radek and John W. Davis. *$1.50.*

INTERNATIONAL SECURITY, by Philip C. Jessup. *$1.50.*

ORES AND INDUSTRY IN SOUTH AMERICA, by H. Foster Bain and Thomas Thornton Read. *$3.50.*

ORES AND INDUSTRY IN THE FAR EAST, by H. Foster Bain (*revised and enlarged edition*). *$3.00.*

THE RECOVERY OF GERMANY, by James W. Angell. *$4.00.*

EUROPE: THE WORLD'S BANKER, 1870–1914, by Herbert Feis. *$5.00.*

DIRECTORY OF AMERICAN AGENCIES CONCERNED WITH THE STUDY OF INTERNATIONAL AFFAIRS, compiled by Ruth Savord. *$1.75.*

FOREWORD

This study has been prepared for submission to the Eighth International Studies Conference, scheduled to meet in London on June 3, 1935, to consider the question of Collective Security. The work has been done under the general direction of a committee composed as follows: Allen W. Dulles (*Chairman*), William O. Scroggs (*Secretary*), Philip C. Jessup (*Rapporteur*), Isaiah Bowman, Raymond Leslie Buell, Joseph P. Chamberlain, Tyler Dennett, Edwin F. Gay, Admiral William V. Pratt, De-Witt C. Poole, James T. Shotwell, General George S. Simonds, Quincy Wright.

This committee was appointed by the Council on Foreign Relations, acting as the National Coördinating Center in the United States for organizations engaged in the study of international relations. The Rapporteur has been charged with the collection of material and the actual preparation of the Report.

The members of the committee participated in mapping out the general plan and subsequently have contributed valuable suggestions and criticisms. They have not sought to control the opinions of the Rapporteur, and he alone is responsible for statements of fact and expressions of opinion contained herein. While the members of the committee, therefore, are not to be understood as necessarily approving or endorsing the contents of this Report, it is submitted under their ægis as a study of the rôle which the United States may be expected to play in contributing toward the stabilization of peace.

In approaching the broad problem of Collective Security, the committee has been inspired by the conviction that it would be futile, indeed even impertinent, for a group of this character to attempt to set forth a program which might be ideal in theory but which could not conceivably receive the support of the government of the United States and which would therefore necessarily be addressed by way of advice to the governments or peoples of other countries. For this reason, the Report is directed toward an analysis of the problem from the point of view of the United States. Theoretical desiderata have not been excluded from consideration, but the guiding principle has been the realistic one of the practicability of proposals from the point of view of actual conditions in the United States and future developments in so far as they can be predicted with some degree of assurance.

The Report is divided into two parts. Part I is historical in its nature, surveying events in the foreign policy of the United States from 1919 to 1935 in order to present a background against which the present situation can be effectively analyzed. Part II is analytical and argumentative in character, devoting consideration to various fields in which the foreign policy of the United States might operate in such a way as to assist or hinder the attainment of Collective Security.

It is always difficult to appraise public opinion. The difficulty is enhanced in the United States, where opinion in the forty-eight states is rarely unanimous on any issue. The difficulties are still greater in respect of issues of foreign policy because large numbers of citizens of the United States are not well informed on international questions and are largely indifferent to them. Many such people acquire through their environment or accept through parental influence, a general point of view which may be described as nationalistic or isolationist on the one hand and as internationalistic on the other hand. Against this very vague and uncomprehending background of so general a notion, all proposals are wont to be measured. Any proposal contemplating international coöperation is rejected *a priori* by the one group and welcomed by the other. No doubt American public opinion is better in-formed to-day than it was twenty years ago. Organiza-tions such as the Council on Foreign Relations, the For-eign Policy Association, the World Peace Foundation, the Carnegie Endowment for International Peace, and the League of Nations Association have largely contrib-uted to this result not only by direct influence upon their members, readers and radio listeners but also indirectly through their influence upon newspaper editors. Circum-stances have also contributed toward increasing the amount of foreign news and comment in the daily press and in periodical literature.

Account must also be taken of the not inconsiderable body of opinion which readily follows party leadership, the editorial policy of a favorite newspaper or the ob-servations of a trusted writer in the daily press, such as Walter Lippmann, Frank Kent or Frank Simonds. In-fluential also are the numerous organizations of men and women, whether political, social, religious or educational, which make the study of foreign affairs an important part of their program through periodic meetings, radio broadcasts or the distribution of printed matter. It is not always easy to draw the line between propaganda and education but if without reproachful connotation these groups may be placed in the propagandist class, it must be noted that international affairs have achieved a place of rapidly increasing prominence in the curricula of schools, colleges, and universities.

In the following survey of the American attitude toward certain aspects of international affairs an attempt has been made to appraise the official attitude of the government as expressed chiefly through its executive branch; the attitude of Senators and Representatives, partly as indicative of official attitudes and partly as re-flective of public opinion among their constituents; the attitude of large groups of persons made vocal through private organizations; and the attitude of expert opinion as revealed in the writings of jurists, scholars, and publicists.

It should be emphasized that this survey does not purport to be a complete history of the foreign policy of the United States, even during a limited period of time. The selection of incidents and expressions of opinion has been guided by a desire to adduce illustrations which are indicative of attitudes and trends.

The Rapporteur gratefully acknowledges the assistance of members of the Committee; of the staff of the Council on Foreign Relations; and of Mr. Ralph Seward and Mr. John C. Crighton, Jr., who assembled much of the material utilized in Part I.

P. C. J.

March 1, 1935.

CONTENTS

INTRODUCTION

In the chapters which follow, attention is focused on American reactions to various plans and proposals which have been put forward in the last fifteen years with a view to improving the means for preventing war. It may be useful as a prelude to this study of the American attitude to give a bird's-eye view of what these plans and proposals are and how they fit into the general world situation.

In looking back over the history of the 19th century and of the first fourteen years of the present century, it will be found that there was then no world-wide organization for keeping the peace. In Europe, at different periods, the Great Powers acted together in order to prevent the outbreak of war. In many cases their efforts were directed toward assuring their own supremacy and preventing the smaller states from taking any action which might prove troublesome to their more powerful neighbors. These combinations of the Great Powers of Europe were variously known as the Holy Alliance and the Concert of Europe; still more indefinitely, they operated on the basis of a general political theory known as the Balance of Power.

In the Western Hemisphere, the United States, largely in pursuance of its traditional policy, commonly known as the Monroe Doctrine, occupied a dominating position which was frequently resented by the smaller states of Central and South America. The Pan American Union was not permitted to develop along political lines. In Asia, the United States and the Great Powers of Europe occasionally acted together as they did at the time of the Boxer Rebellion in 1901. On other occasions, they found a unifying principle in the policy of the Open Door, which was intended to secure equal opportunities for the trade and commerce of all nations. Nevertheless, there were often signs that Japan sought a position of dominance in the East comparable to that which the United States occupied in the Western Hemisphere.

As early as 1899, when the First Peace Conference met at The Hague, there was apparent a belief that the whole world was interdependent in so far as the problem of war and peace was concerned. Mr. Holls, one of the American delegates to that Conference, remarked, in commenting on the treaties there signed: "Modern states cannot remain indifferent to international conflicts, no matter where they may arise, and who may be the parties. Under present conditions, war, though between two states only, must be regarded as an international evil, which should be prevented wherever possible, by international means." Although this idea was accepted, The Hague Conferences did not succeed in establishing any world-wide machinery which could translate the idea into action.

At the close of the World War, chiefly under the inspiration of President Woodrow Wilson, an attempt was made to provide a world-wide peace machinery through the establishment of the League of Nations. Article 11 of the League Covenant furnishes a key to the theory underlying the League system: "Any war or threat of war, whether immediately affecting any of the Members of the League or not, is hereby declared a matter of concern to the whole League. . ."

In support of this theory, the states agreed upon an international organization and procedures to make it operate effectively. The Covenant provides for the creation of an Assembly in which all Members are represented; for a Council in which a smaller group of powers are represented and which serves as an executive committee; and for a Secretariat which furnishes a permanent administrative and research staff.

Without attempting to go into great detail, we may note certain outstanding aspects of the League peace system. By Article 10, Members of the League "undertake to respect and preserve as against external aggression the territorial integrity and existing political independence of all Members of the League." Under Article 11, it is "the friendly right" of each League Member to call the attention of the Assembly or the Council to "any circumstance whatever affecting international relations which threatens to disturb international peace or the good understanding between nations upon which peace depends." By Article 12, the Members agree that they will submit any dispute either to arbitration or judicial settlement or to inquiry by the Council and that they will not resort to war until three months after the award, decision or report.

Article 13 covers justiciable disputes and provides that the Members will carry out any award or decision and "that they will not resort to war against a Member of the League which complies therewith." Types of disputes which are not suitable for submission to arbitration or judicial settlement, are, according to Article 15, to be submitted to the Council for investigation. If the Council makes a unanimous report, the Members agree not to go to war with any party to the dispute which complies with the recommendations of the report. If the report is not unanimous, the Members are free to take such action as they consider proper. The Council may refer disputes to the Assembly, which will then act in the same way as the Council would have acted.

Article 16 is the article which contains the provisions for "sanctions." It begins as follows: "Should any Member of the League resort to war in disregard of its covenants under Articles 12, 13 or 15, it shall *ipso facto* be deemed to have committed an act of war against all other Members of the League, which hereby undertake immediately to subject it to the severance of all trade or financial relations, the prohibition of all intercourse between their nationals and the nationals of the covenant-breaking State, and the prevention of all financial, commercial or personal intercourse between the nationals of the covenant-breaking State and the nationals of any other State, whether a Member of the League or not." The Council has the duty of recommending what steps shall be taken and the Members of the League agree to assist each other in the application of these sanctions.

The gist of all these provisions is that League Members agree to settle their disputes peacefully and to allow all of them to be investigated by some kind of an international body.[1] However, there are certain "gaps" in the Covenant which make it possible in certain situations for a Member of the League to go to war without having violated its obligations under the Covenant. It should also be noted that under the Covenant the Council does not have the power to render a final and binding decision as to a violation of the Covenant and it cannot order the Members of the League to take any particular military, naval, or economic steps in connection with the application of sanctions.

The United States, Russia and other states did not become Members of the League and the League did not therefore become a universal association as had been hoped. Since its creation, the League has been feeling its way along untried paths, attempting from time to time to remedy defects in the Covenant and to fill its gaps.

One of the first steps taken by the League, was to set up the Permanent Court of International Justice, as provided for in Article 14 of the Covenant. A number of prior attempts to create such a permanent court had failed

---

[1] There is a reservation, under Article 15, of questions which are purely domestic.

because the large and small states could not agree upon a method of selecting judges. This difficulty was met by the use of the new League machinery; the Council and Assembly act as electoral bodies, voting separately but simultaneously upon a list of nominees supplied by the various national groups which make up the panel of the old Hague Court of Arbitration.[2] The plan has given satisfaction to both large and small states and has worked well in practice. The Court has been functioning for fourteen years and has dealt with almost fifty cases. Forty-nine states are now parties to the treaty under which the Court was established and functions.

The basic treaty, or statute, of the Court gives the tribunal no jurisdiction of any case except by the consent of both parties to the dispute. However, forty-one states are now bound by a separate agreement, known as the Optional Clause, whereby they agree in advance that the Court shall have jurisdiction in certain categories of disputes. The Court also has the power to render advisory opinions on legal questions submitted to it by the Council or Assembly of the League. In practice, this function has proved to be extremely useful and has been exercised in a strictly judicial manner.

In 1923, President Harding asked the consent of the United States Senate to ratify the treaty of this World Court. The Senate did not act until 1926 when it gave its consent, subject to five reservations. These reservations not being wholly acceptable to the other governments, a new treaty was negotiated in 1929 by Mr. Elihu Root, to provide for their acceptance and application. The Senate finally voted on this new treaty on January 29, 1935; and as there were seven votes less than the two-

[2] This solution was proposed by Mr. Elihu Root who was a member of the Committee of Jurists which was invited by the Council to draw up a plan for the Court.

thirds necessary to give approval, the President was unable to ratify the World Court treaty.

The second important step taken by the League was in pursuance of Article 8 of the Covenant whereby the Members recognized "that the maintenance of peace requires the reduction of national armaments to the lowest point consistent with national safety and the enforcement by common action of international obligations." Committees were set up to study the problem. It became apparent at once that the questions of disarmament and political security were inextricably mingled and that treaties which would guarantee security must take precedence.

Meanwhile, the government of the United States took the initiative by convening the Washington Conference on the Limitation of Armament, which met from November, 1921, to February, 1922. At this Conference, a naval limitation treaty was signed by the United States, Great Britain, Japan, France and Italy. It limited the construction of certain types of warships and set up the famous 5-5-3 ratio as a measure of American, British and Japanese naval strength. The ratio was adopted, not on any theory of inequality between Japan and the other two powers, but as a recognition and description of the situation which then existed. The naval treaty was accompanied and made possible by two political treaties. The Four-Power Treaty between the United States, Great Britain, Japan and France guaranteed their respective insular possessions in the Pacific and called a halt to their continued fortification. It provided also for the termination of the Anglo-Japanese Alliance. The Nine-Power Treaty included the same four states, plus China, Belgium, Portugal, The Netherlands and Italy. It dealt particularly with China and contained agreements to respect Chinese sovereignty and territorial integrity.

The next important step in the activities of the League is found in the preparation during 1922-23, of a Draft Treaty of Mutual Assistance. This draft treaty declared that "aggressive war is an international crime." It sought to strengthen the League system for the prevention of war, by giving greater powers to the Council. The Council was authorized to apply sanctions, even at a stage when hostilities were merely threatened and had not actually broken out. The Council could require Members of the League to contribute in specified ways to make the sanctions effective. "Aggression" was not defined, but suggestions on this point were drawn up separately. There were also very general provisions regarding disarmament. This draft treaty was opposed by the British and other governments, and was never adopted.

The League continued its efforts largely on the basis of M. Herriot's declaration that arbitration, security and disarmament were inseparable. Again the scene shifted to the United States, where a private American group, including Professor James T. Shotwell, General Tasker H. Bliss, Mr. David Hunter Miller and others, prepared a new draft treaty on disarmament and security, which has come to be known as the American or Shotwell plan. This plan built upon the Draft Treaty of Mutual Assistance, but sought to fill an important gap by defining "aggression." Under its terms a state which refused to submit a dispute to the Permanent Court of International Justice, or which engaged in war for any purpose other than defense, would be an aggressor.

This plan was not accepted by the League but was used in connection with a new League project known as the Geneva Protocol of 1924. This Protocol again denounced aggressive war, and sought to close the "gaps" in the Covenant so that war would always be illegal.

Arbitration was compulsory, as under the American plan. Any state which resorted to force without exhausting the pacific procedures outlined in the Protocol, would be presumed guilty of aggression. The Council, if unanimous, could pronounce final judgment on this point. The application of sanctions was not left uncertain, as under Article 16 of the Covenant, but was made nearly automatic. Each state was left the judge of the way in which it should carry out its obligations to apply sanctions, but the Council would have the power to decide when those obligations existed. The British government was again found in opposition to this plan, and the Protocol failed of adoption.

In 1925, a new type of partial solution to the problems of security and peace preservation was provided in the form of the Locarno agreements. These agreements were concluded outside the League but were closely related to League machinery and led to Germany's joining the League. The principal treaty was the security and guarantee pact between Great Britain, France, Belgium, Italy and Germany, which sought particularly to guarantee France against invasion by Germany. Subsidiary agreements were concluded between Germany and her Eastern neighbors.

In the same year, the League Council set up a Preparatory Commission for the Disarmament Conference which proceeded to detailed studies of technical disarmament problems. A first practical step was also taken in the conclusion of a convention to regulate the traffic in arms. A preliminary move in this direction had been taken by the conclusion of the treaty of St. Germain in 1919, but by 1925 only eleven governments had ratified this treaty. The more important governments took the position that they could not ratify unless the United States did so, since the United States was one of the leading countries in the manufacture and export of arms and munitions. The United States accepted the invitation to be represented at the Conference which drew up the 1925 convention. This treaty subjected all international arms shipments to a licensing system, and forbade sales to private persons; sales to governments were not restricted.

In 1927, a parallel League Committee on Arbitration and Security was created and began work on the other two facets of the disarmament problem. The work of the committee led to the formulation, in 1928, of the General Act for the Pacific Settlement of International Disputes. This General Act was in substance a model convention designed to unify agreements for conciliation, arbitration, and judicial settlement. It was accompanied by model bipartite treaties which states could accept if they preferred. The same committee prepared model treaties of mutual assistance and non-aggression, based largely on the Locarno plan. These were recommended to Members of the League as likely to contribute to the peace of Europe.

In 1928, also, the Briand-Kellogg Pact was signed. It came into force the following year and exists as the most widely accepted treaty designed to stabilize the peace of the world. The first steps toward its negotiation were taken by the French government, but in its final form it is commonly regarded as an American contribution. It contains only two substantive articles which are terse and clear, requiring no paraphrase or commentary at this point:

Article 1

The High Contracting Parties solemnly declare in the names of their respective peoples that they condemn recourse to war for the solution of international controversies, and renounce it as an instrument of national policy in their relations with one another.

Article 2

The High Contracting Parties agree that the settlement or solution of all disputes or conflicts of whatever nature or of whatever origin they may be, which may arise among them, shall never be sought except by pacific means.

In 1930, a further model treaty was proposed; a draft of it had been considered by the League Assembly in 1928. This new plan was known as the Draft Convention to strengthen the Means of preventing War. Under this Convention, states would agree in advance to comply with proposals made by the League Council for the settlement of disputes or to avoid aggravating them, and to abstain from any measures which would hinder an adjustment. If hostilities had actually begun, the contracting parties would agree to accept the recommendations of the Council regarding the cessation of hostilities or the creation of a demilitarized zone.

In the meantime, the Preparatory Commission for the Disarmament Conference was struggling through the mazes of military, naval and air technicalities. The Conference finally met at Geneva on February 2, 1932, with representatives of fifty-nine countries present. It held general meetings also in 1933 and 1934, and between meetings it functioned through its committees. It has proved repeatedly that disarmament can not be considered apart from security. The proposals for achieving security have ranged all the way from bare consultative pacts to international police forces. At the time of this writing no disarmament treaty has been signed.

The foregoing outline does not, of course, give even a general picture of all the activities of the League of Nations. In the interests of clarity, it has excluded everything which does not bear directly upon the history of American relations to the cause of the stabilization of peace. It has excluded also a description of the chain of events against which the world's peace machinery has been tested. It has not sought to point out the effect of recent German policy; of the realignment of Soviet foreign policy; of the Franco-Italian rapprochement and the Eastern Locarnos. All these matters are relevant to a full understanding of the problem of collective security, but they escape the compass of this book.

PART I

HISTORICAL SUMMARY OF THE ATTITUDE OF THE UNITED STATES FROM 1919 TO 1935

CHAPTER ONE

THE LEAGUE OF NATIONS

The Reception of the Covenant

It is important to recall the reception given to the Covenant of the League of Nations in the United States, because that original reception has colored a large section of American public opinion ever since. The Republican party, which opposed President Wilson's proposal for the creation of the League, elevated what began largely as a political controversy into a major policy of the party. The Democratic party, which came back into power with the elections of 1932 after an interval of twelve years, was divided in its adherence to Wilsonian international policy, and on taking office was so beset with the domestic emergency that until very recently it has given little evidence of an intention to reëspouse that policy. Although the two parties have been drawing closer together on these issues and are not at present far apart in their basic attitudes, the bitterness of the original political conflict over the League is not yet eliminated as a factor in public opinion.

There is the usual danger of over-simplification in stressing the rôle played by the League issue in the American presidential elections of 1920. President Wilson and his party were opposed also on many domestic issues—tariff, income tax, banking, and the general question of increased executive power. There was, moreover, a natural swing back to the strong Republican party whose candidate, Hughes, had polled only 600,000 fewer votes than Wilson in 1916. President Wilson's stubborn refusal to submit the Covenant of the League to the Senate separately from the rest of the Peace Treaty not only caused further irritation in the Senate but rallied against the League those who were opposed to other portions of the Treaty of Versailles.

"The Republican majority" in 1920, according to Walter Lippmann, "was composed of men and women who thought a Republican victory would kill the League, plus those who thought it was the most peaceful way to secure the League, plus those who thought it the surest way offered to obtain an amended League. All of these voters were inextricably entangled with their own desire, or the desire of other voters to improve business, or put labor in its place, or to punish the Democrats for going to war, or to punish them for not having gone sooner, or to get rid of Mr. Burleson, or to improve the price of wheat, or to lower taxes, or to stop Mr. Daniels from outbuilding the (naval) world, or to help Mr. Harding do the same thing."[1]

Yet from this confusion of issues and motives, the successful Republican party was able to convince the country that the election was a mandate of the American people against entering the League of Nations.[2] This is the more surprising in view of the attitude of thirty of the most prominent members of the Republican party, who during the campaign issued a public statement voicing their opinion that the election of Mr. Harding was the surest road to lead the United States into an association of nations. Although this plea has been denounced as evidently unsound and misleading, it was animated, at least in the minds of some of the signers, by the conviction that the new Senate would still contain enough Republicans who would block a Democratic President's proposals for entering the League, even with reserva-

[1] Walter Lippmann, Public Opinion (1922), 195-6.
[2] Even the arch-opponent of the League, Senator Henry Cabot Lodge of Massachusetts, admitted that as late as May 1, 1919, the masses of the people as well as the leaders of opinion were in favor of the League. H. C. Lodge, The Senate and the League of Nations (1925), 147-8.

tions, whereas the same Republican Senators could be induced to uphold a Republican President's appeal for ratification of the treaty with reservations.[3]
There can be no doubt that great numbers of Americans became imbued with utterly false notions about the League as a result of campaign oratory and literature which is notoriously unreliable and unvaryingly accepted by those who wish to believe. The League was represented as a superstate; membership in it as a total abdication of the sovereignty and independence of the United States. The League would abolish American tariffs for the benefit of foreigners; the United States would be forced to accept unlimited Oriental immigration; despite the vague and inaccurate words finally inserted in Article 21 of the Covenant, the Monroe Doctrine would be nullified. Worst of all, said the orators, the youth of the United States would be summoned at the beck and call of the League—where the British Empire was represented as having six votes to our one—to fight foreign wars in all quarters of the globe.

Of course, those voters who accepted this unreal interpretation of the Covenant voted against the party which advocated American membership. The same result would have followed in every country if such representations had been true or had been believed.

The citizens who favored the League Covenant included large numbers of persons enrolled in various peace societies and particularly large numbers of persons connected with religious organizations. The American League to Enforce Peace, under the leadership of ex-President Taft, had attracted many prominent citizens to its ranks. The women's organizations, which subse-

_____

[3] On this entire contest, the most useful single source is D. F. Fleming, *The United States and the League of Nations* (1932), *passim.* See also Charles P. Howland (ed.), *Survey of American Foreign Relations*, 1928, 254-283.

quently exercised very great influence in the peace movement, were not yet effective in the political field, since
the 19th Amendment to the Constitution, which gave
them the suffrage, did not come into effect until August
26, 1920, and no very large number of this new body of
voters made their voice felt in the elections of the following November. Moreover, as indicated above in the
analysis of the votes of that year, the peace forces were
split wide open by the perplexing volume of reservations
and the disagreement in the ranks of the leaders.

In the Senate, opposition had been focused chiefly on
Article 10 of the Covenant, which was interpreted as an
absolute guarantee to defend by the armed forces of the
United States the territorial integrity of every member
of the League. Specific examples of such obligations
were suggested: aiding Great Britain to put down rebellion in Ireland (an appeal to the Irish vote); preventing
China from ever recovering Shantung; perpetually
trying to keep the peace in a completely Balkanized
Europe; perpetuating every injustice contained in the
peace treaties. It was chiefly the vagueness and uncer-
tainty of this commitment which caused alarm, as is
indicated by the fact that at one point during the Senate
debates the Republicans were willing to accept the proposed tripartite treaty whereby Great Britain and the
United States would have guaranteed the security of
France, provided President Wilson would submit this
treaty separately, which he refused to do.

To guard against the imagined dangers of Article 10,
the second of the fifteen Lodge [4] reservations provided:

---

[4] Senator Henry Cabot Lodge of Massachusetts was at the time the
Chairman of the Foreign Relations Committee of the Senate. This position is one of enormous influence in all matters dealing with American
foreign relations. As the bitter personal and political opponent of
President Wilson and in his official position, Senator Lodge led the fight
against the Covenant, and the reservations on which the debates centered
are commonly known by his name.

The United States assumes no obligation to preserve the territorial integrity or political independence of any other country by
the employment of its military or naval forces, its resources, or
any form of economic discrimination, or to interfere in any way
in controversies between nations, including all controversies relating to territorial integrity or political independence, whether
members of the League or not, under the provisions of Article 10,
or to employ the military or naval forces of the United States, under any article of the treaty for any purpose, unless in any particular case the Congress, which, under the Constitution, has the
sole power to declare war or authorize the employment of the
military or naval forces of the United States, shall, in the exercise
of full liberty of action, by act or joint resolution so provide.[5]

Senator Hitchcock (Democrat) offered a substitute reservation, which President Wilson was willing to accept,
as follows:

That the advice mentioned in Article 10 of the Covenant of the
League which the Council may give to the member nations as to
the employment of their naval and military forces is merely advice
which each member nation is free to accept or reject according to
the convenience and judgment of its then existing government,
and in the United States this advice can only be accepted by action
of the Congress at the time in being, Congress alone under the
Constitution of the United States having the power to declare
war.[6]

This point of view with regard to the supposed obligations of Article 10 is important because it has been
a dominant theme in the American attitude ever since—
an absolute refusal to yield to any international body the
power to decide when the United States shall act upon
any obligation which it may have assumed. As will be
noted later, this attitude extends even to a decision upon
the question whether the circumstances bring the obligation into effect, for example, under arbitration treaties.[7]
So with reference to other articles of the Covenant and

[5] *Congressional Record*, LIX, pt. 5, 4333.
[6] *Ibid.*, 4331.
[7] *Vide infra*, p. 82.

as a safeguard under paragraph 8 of Article 15, the fourth Lodge reservation declared:

> The United States reserves to itself exclusively the right to decide what questions are within its domestic jurisdiction and declares that all domestic and political questions relating wholly or in part to its internal affairs, including immigration, labor, coastwise traffic, the tariff, commerce, the suppression of traffic in women and children and in opium and other dangerous drugs, and all other domestic questions, are solely within the jurisdiction of the United States and are not under this treaty to be submitted in any way either to arbitration or to the consideration of the Council or of the Assembly of the League of Nations, or any agency thereof, or to the decision or recommendation of any other Power.[8]

Similarly, the first Lodge reservation, with reference to the right of withdrawal, insisted that "the United States shall be the sole judge as to whether all its international obligations and all its obligations under the said Covenant have been fulfilled, and notice of withdrawal by the United States may be given by a concurrent resolution of the Congress of the United States."[9]

Although in the debate on the Covenant of the League the fear of a superstate was undoubtedly present, reservations of this type represent a more general objection, based on Congressional jealousy of its prerogatives.[10] This struggle between the executive and legislative branches (particularly the Senate) of the United States government is one of the chief factors in American foreign policy and must be kept in mind constantly. It was the failure to realize this which made the Senate's re-

---

[8] *Congressional Record*, LIX, pt. 4, 3741.
[9] *Ibid.*, 3242.
[10] Cf. Reservation No. 7 requiring Congressional sanction of the appointment of any American representative on any League body and Reservation No. 9 disclaiming any financial obligation of the United States to contribute to League expenses before Congress had appropriated the funds. *Ibid.*, pt. 6, 5422, and pt. 4, 3943.

pudiation of President Wilson's treaty so great a blow to the peoples of Europe. Coupled with the constitutional rule requiring a two-thirds vote of the Senate for the approval of any treaty, this factor places a severe limitation on the United States in the conduct of its foreign relations.[11] Whether it is a beneficial or a detrimental aspect of the American governmental system need not be explored here but neither the constitutional two-thirds rule nor the traditional jealousy between Senate and President is likely to be eliminated in the near future and this fact is of great importance to this study.

The reservation to Article 10 was apparently considered broad enough to afford protection to the United States against the application of the "sanction" articles of the Covenant but a particular reservation to Article 16 should be noted:

> The United States reserves the right to permit, in its discretion, the nationals of a Covenant-breaking state, as defined in Article 16 of the Covenant of the League of Nations, residing within the United States, or in countries other than that violating said Article 16, to continue their commercial, financial and personal relations with the nationals of the United States.[12]

There were other reservations but they add little to the general picture drawn here, except to deepen the shadows and intensify the highlights.

Summing up, it must be reiterated that no single factor brought about the defeat of the League Covenant in the United States and it would therefore be a mistake to make too dogmatic an analysis. One may attempt to segregate some of the issues which remained to condition

[11] See D. F. Fleming, *The Treaty Veto of the American Senate* (1930), and P. C. Jessup, "List of Unperfected Treaties," *American Journal of International Law*, XXVII, 138-9, January, 1933; R. J. Dangerfield, *In Defense of the Senate* (1933); Howland, *op. cit.*, 83-148.
[12] No. 11 of the Lodge Reservations: *Congressional Record*, LIX, pt. 6, 5423.

American foreign policy from those which were temporary.

It was the League as a superstate which was opposed so violently in the United States. Such a League was a ghostly spectre which never had any existence in fact but the superstition strongly persists in American thought. There is a hostility deep-rooted in large sections of American opinion toward the acceptance of any obligation which would compel the United States to participate in any international repressive or punitive measures as a result of an engagement made in advance of the event.

There is a rather unreasoning and beclouded devotion to the Monroe Doctrine (the meaning of which is obscure to most), but a devotion which stems from a traditional attachment almost religious in its fervor.

There is a potent unwillingness in the Senate to entrust broad authority in international affairs to the executive. (The trends during the present Roosevelt administration will be considered later.)[13]

Except in times of national emergency, there is little adherence to the assertion of Daniel Webster that politics stop at the water's edge.[14] While an unpopular foreign policy is a vulnerable point of attack for a party's political opponents, few votes are gained by even the most successful ventures in foreign affairs. This attitude of the American electorate tends to discourage politicians from supporting new departures in foreign policy and

---

[13] *Vide infra,* p. 128.

[14] Professor C. A. Beard, in his recent book entitled *The Idea of National Interest,* develops the theme that, from the earliest days of the Republic, foreign policy has been a real issue between the two major parties. He traces the divergent views from the agrarianism of Jefferson and the industrialism of Hamilton up through the imperialism of McKinley (representing the industrial east) and the anti-imperialism of Bryan (representing the agricultural middle west). He finds a more or less continuing thread running up to the present time. It may be fair to say that the average voter in the United States has not always been conscious of the immediate importance or consistency of these issues throughout American history.

helps to explain the success of such attacks as those on the League of Nations and the World Court.

There is a very considerable body of idealistic opinion which, however, is only occasionally translated into effective political action.

After this sketch of the background of the American attitude toward the League of Nations, the subsequent relations between the government of the United States and the League may be explored.

Subsequent Relations between the United States and the League of Nations

During the campaign of 1920 the Republican candidate for the presidency, Mr. Harding, declared that if he were elected he would summon "the best minds in America, representing an all-American opinion, to consult and advise as to America's relationship to the present association of nations, to modifications of it or substitutes for it." [15]   But in his first message to Congress President Harding said, "In the existing League of Nations with its super-powers, this Republic will have no part." Apparently this was taken by the Department of State under Secretary Hughes as a rigorously literal enunciation of policy, since during the six months following Harding's inauguration the Department did not even acknowledge communications received from the Secretary General of the League.   Following numerous private protests against the discourtesy of this attitude, the Department of State began in the fall of 1921 to send formal acknowledgments of communications from the League.   These acknowledgments usually contained a stock phrase: "The Secretary of State has taken note of this information for any purposes of relevancy to the

[15] J. W. Garner, *American Foreign Policies* (1928), 192.

United States as a state not a member of the League of Nations."[16]

This official attitude was in line with that of various Senators and sections of American opinion which seemed to feel that the Republican party had killed the League. Perhaps they had scotched the snake, but they had not killed it. By constant reiteration of the allegation, "The League is dead," they fondly hoped that their wish would come true. The wish was father to the thought, but the thought had no factual children.

Beginning in 1923, a change could be detected in the official policy of the United States toward the League. Unofficial observers acting in a "consultative capacity" represented the United States at such non-political League conferences as those which dealt with opium, obscene publications, transit and communications, and customs formalities. In the fall of 1924, under the authorization of a joint resolution of Congress, an official delegation was sent by the United States to attend the Second Opium Conference.

The ice having been broken, the United States from that time on did not hesitate to send official delegations to non-political conferences in which it was interested. Nevertheless, the practice of sending merely observers and experts who were to act in an advisory capacity continued over many years. As late as February, 1930, when the League summoned a tariff conference to meet in Geneva, the Department of State informed the Secretary General that, while it sympathized with the objectives of

---

[16] See Raymond B. Fosdick, "The State Department and the League of Nations," *American Review of Reviews*, April 1924, LXIX, 178-82. In general for this section the following two studies and the references cited therein have been utilized: R. L. Buell, "The United States and the League of Nations, *Foreign Policy Association, Information Service,* VI, No. 9, July 9, 1930; U. P. Hubbard, "The Coöperation of the United States with the League of Nations and with the International Labour Organization," *International Conciliation,* No. 274, November, 1931.

the conference, it could not at that time "usefully participate in the conference." This was not particularly significant since a number of states members of the League
also declined to participate. The State Department did
instruct the first secretary of the Paris Embassy "to associate himself with the Consulate in Geneva, with a
view to obtaining information regarding the developments
of the conference." [17]

The great change which had taken place in the official
attitude is shown by two pronouncements of the Republican party in 1928. The Republican platform declared:

This Government has definitely refused membership in the
League of Nations and to assume any obligations under the
covenant of the League. On this we stand.

In accordance, however, with the long-established American
practice of giving aid and assistance to other peoples, we have
most usefully assisted by coöperation in the humanitarian and
technical work undertaken by the League, without involving ourselves in European politics by accepting membership.

In his acceptance speech of August 11, 1928, Mr. Hoover
stood on this same position. In a bulletin issued by the
Republican National Committee during the campaign,
Secretary Kellogg described the attitude of the United
States toward coöperation with the League in the fol-
lowing words:

The Government of the United States has continued its policy
of friendly and helpful coöperation with the League of Nations
on subjects of international humanitarian concern. . . . The
correspondence with the League is carried on by the American
Legation at Berne. Information on the activities of the League in
which this Government is not directly represented is obtained
through the Consulate in Geneva. The willingness of the United
States to coöperate freely, fully and helpfully with the League
in matters of genuine international concern and our Government's

---

[17] Hubbard, *op. cit.,* 714.

determination to adhere to the policy of non-participation in the League itself is now well understood at Geneva.[18]

Meanwhile, numbers of American citizens, acting in their private capacities, served on numerous League committees as experts. Some of these individuals occupied positions in the United States government but their services were not rendered in their official capacities. The first general League convention which was adhered to by the United States was the Convention on Slavery and Forced Labor, which was approved by the Senate on February 25, 1929. The historic interest in the United States in the question of the suppression of slavery, based largely on religious and humanitarian grounds, was influential in securing the approval of this convention. When he transmitted the treaty to the Senate, the President included a letter from Secretary Kellogg in which Mr. Kellogg said that "as the functions exercised by the Secretary General of the League of Nations" under the treaty "are merely those of a depositary and of a transmitting agency, it is not considered that it would be necessary that accession to the convention by the United States be made subject to a reservation indicating the position of this Government with respect to the League. If, however, the Senate should consider that a reservation on this point is desirable, one might be made."[19]   The Senate did not consider a League reservation necessary, and the accession of the United States was deposited with the League on March 21, 1929.[20]

The gradual development in the attitude of the United States Department of State toward matters connected with the League of Nations should not be attributed particularly to pressure from pro-League groups or to

---

[18] Frank B. Kellogg, "Foreign Relations," Republican National Committee, Bulletin No. 5, 1928, 13.

[19] *Congressional Record*, LXX, No. 64, February 25, 1929.

[20] United States Treaty Series No. 778.

any feeling in official quarters that public opinion throughout the country had become "pro-League." The change was rather due to a natural and almost inevitable evolution. The blunt discourtesy of the attitude taken in 1921 was the consequence of the extremely bitter feeling in the Republican party during 1919 and may be attributed particularly to the arrogant assurance bred of the sweeping political victory over the Democratic party at the polls in November, 1920. However, the United States had to continue dealing with the rest of the world in matters of common concern. When it appeared that the other governments were unwilling to handle these problems by the old clumsy method of individual correspondence and discussion, it became obvious that the United States would have to fall in with the more efficient conference method which was being rapidly developed in the post-war period.

The United States of course was no stranger to the conference method. It had utilized it to the full in Pan American affairs and had not hesitated to participate in such conferences as those at the Hague in 1899 and 1907 and even in the more distinctly political conference of Algeciras in 1906, as well as conferences in the non-political field such as the International Opium Conference of 1912.

The utility of an international agency for the preparation and organization of such conferences had been recognized in the use of the Bureau of the Pan American Union. Secretary of State Bryan had stated the point clearly on January 31, 1914, in a circular instruction to American diplomatic officers regarding a call for a third Hague Peace Conference. He suggested that the Administrative Council of the Permanent Court of Arbitration at the Hague might well serve as an agency through which the governments might operate. "To this council," he said, "the task of preparation for the conference may readily and appropriately be committed. The place at which the Council sits leaves nothing to be desired from the point of view of convenience, while the entrusting of the work to a competent body already in existence would result in an appreciable saving both in time and in expense."[21] Along the same lines, Mr. Charles Evans Hughes in a speech at the New York Republican State Convention April 15, 1924, referring to the utilizing of the League facilities in organizing conferences, said: "There is no more difficulty in dealing with the organization of the League in this way for the purpose of protecting our interests or following our policies than there would be in dealing with the British Empire."

As this process of non-political coöperation continued, the country at large, and particularly the Senate, gradually became accustomed to this type of coöperation and ceased being disturbed by the fact that representatives of the United States were attending a meeting in the city of Geneva.

The trend of development is well illustrated by the course of United States practice on a point of relatively minor importance. On July 16, 1920, the governments of states not members of the League were invited to register their treaties in the League Treaty Series. The German and Ecuadorian governments accepted this invitation but the United States apparently did not even reply to the invitation. In 1925 the United States government advised the Secretary General of the League that it would thenceforth send to the Secretariat treaties contracted by the government of the United States. Accordingly, on February 3, 1926, the Secretary General announced that "such treaties, if not otherwise previously published by the Secretariat, will be included in the

[21] *United States Foreign Relations* (1914), 5.

League Treaty Series with the above explanation, and with the understanding that as the United States is not a member of the League, it does not register them with the Secretariat." [22] On February 27, 1921, Assistant Secretary of State Castle, replying to a letter from Professor Manley O. Hudson, in which Professor Hudson urged that the United States register its treaties, stated that the Department of State felt "that in view of the fact that the United States is not a member of the League of Nations, it would be inappropriate for this government to register treaties with the Secretariat." [23] However, in January, 1934, an arrangement was effected by exchange of notes between the Acting Legal Adviser of the Secretariat of the League and the American Consul at Geneva, whereby the United States agreed to register its treaties subject to the understanding that the United States did not thereby acquiesce in the provisions of Article 18 of the Covenant and accepted no obligation to pay any charge or expenses. [24]

Along political lines, the most striking instances of American coöperation with the League are to be found in the negotiations for the settlement of the Leticia boundary dispute, which nearly led to war between Colombia and Peru in 1932; the war in the Chaco, an area claimed by both Paraguay and Bolivia, whose long dispute finally led to open hostilities in the summer of 1932; and the Sino-Japanese controversy over Manchuria, which came to a head with the Japanese attack on Mukden on

[22] Manley O. Hudson, "The Registration of Treaties of the United States," *American Journal of International Law*, XXII, 852, October 1928.

[23] Hubbard, *op. cit.*, 756.

[24] United States Executive Agreement Series No. 70, effective January 23, 1934. Attention should be called also to the metamorphosis of the American Consulate in Geneva. From a routine consular office it has been transformed into a highly efficient and important liaison office between the United States government and the League. *Cf.* Harold J. Tobin, "The Problem of Permanent Representation at the League of Nations," *Political Science Quarterly* XLVIII, 481, 501-2, December 1933.

the night of September 18, 1931. As will appear from the later consideration of these incidents,[25] these efforts at coöperation were made rather haltingly and their effectiveness was weakened by a lack of consistency. For example, in dealing with the Manchurian crisis, Secretary of State Stimson felt it necessary to proceed with great caution in instructing the American consul at Geneva, Mr. Prentiss Gilbert, to sit in with the Council. Mr. Gilbert was required to fill a rôle reminiscent of the familiar figures of the three little monkeys who represent the three virtues of See no Evil, Hear no Evil, Speak no Evil; Mr. Gilbert was not to see, hear or speak when the other conferees mentioned the Covenant of the League but was charged to exercise all his faculties when the Briand-Kellogg Pact was under discussion. Apparently even this cautious step aroused some opposition among the Senators, with the result that, at the next meeting of the Council in Paris, Ambassador Dawes played a rather farcical rôle, sitting in his hotel while the Council met in another building, with Mr. Arthur Sweetser, the American who was Deputy Chief of the Information Section of the League Secretariat, dashing madly back and forth in an attempt to serve as a liaison officer.

Although there was more drama in the Manchurian crisis, probably the fullest and most effective measure of American political coöperation with the League has been found in the American representation at the Disarmament Conference and on the Preparatory Commission.[26] Under the leadership of Mr. Norman Davis, the United States took full part in the work of the conference and its committees, not hesitating to keep informed and to make its views known even when the most delicate political prob-

[25] *Vide infra*, pp. 43 and 78-80.
[26] *Vide infra*, Chapter III.

lems were under discussion. It was in the course of this participation in the Disarmament Conference that Mr. Davis, on May 22, 1933, made his famous declaration indicating that, if a disarmament treaty were concluded, the United States would at least not put obstacles in the way of League members if they sought to apply sanctions against a Covenant-breaking state in a clear case of aggression.[27]

Throughout the United States some of the peace forces have continued an active campaign to bring about American membership in the League, admitting that some reservations may be necessary. An interesting attempt was made to sample public opinion in the state of Massachusetts, where any "question of public policy" may be put on the official ballot in response to a petition of a certain number of voters, for the purpose of a popular referendum. A question regarding American membership in the League was thus put up to some of the voters of Massachusetts in 1932 and 1934. In 1932, 25,631 votes, or 63.2 per cent of the votes cast, favored joining the League, with 14,879, or 36.8 per cent opposed. On November 6, 1934, the question was voted on in other districts of Massachusetts which were not polled in 1932. In this second referendum 217,421 votes were cast, of which 62.31 per cent were in favor of membership and 37.69 per cent opposed.[28] It is hard to say whether this poll in Massachusetts is typical of the entire country. A good many arguments pro and con can be advanced as to the adequacy of such a test.[28a] Taken in

[27] *Vide infra*, p. 55.

[28] *New York Times*, November 25, 1934.

[28a] It may be noted that both Senators from Massachusetts, in apparent response to pressure from their constituents, voted against ratification of the World Court protocols in January, 1935. Attention may also be called to a recent poll of American colleges and universities, conducted by the *Literary Digest*, which showed 32,404 students in favor of American membership in the League and 32,320 opposed; *New York Times*, February 2, 1935.

its most favorable light, this cannot be regarded as an overwhelming judgment in favor of American membership in the League, but it is undoubtedly true that no such large percentage in favor of joining the League could have been obtained ten or fifteen years ago. It would be folly to ignore the influence of the Hearst press, which continues its rabid campaign against the League.[29] It would also be folly to ignore those large sections of informed American opinion which are also hostile to League membership. There seems to be no question about the continuance of United States coöperation with the League in economic, financial, and humanitarian matters. It seems quite likely also that the United States will on occasion again coöperate with the League in political matters in which the United States is particularly interested. It is also apparent that the present administration is inclined to be more liberal in its international policy than were the preceding administrations. This may be due partly to the Wilsonian heritage and partly to the natural fruition of the progressive development already outlined. Although the general attitude of the Roosevelt administration has been somewhat broader in regard to coöperation with the League, yet it should not be forgotten that in his address before the New York State Grange at Albany on February 2, 1932, Mr. Roosevelt, then Governor of New York, flatly stated that he did not then favor American entry into the League. He pointed out that he had favored such action in 1920 but

The League of Nations to-day is not the League conceived by Woodrow Wilson. It might have been had the United States joined. Too often, through these years, its major function has been not the broad overwhelming purpose of world peace, but rather a mere meeting place for the political discussion of strictly

[29] *Vide infra,* p. 31.

European political national difficulties. In these the United States should have no part.

The fact remains that we did not join the League. The League has not developed through these years along the course contemplated by its founder, nor have the principal members shown a disposition to divert the huge sums spent on armaments into the channels of legitimate trade, balanced budgets and payment of obligations.

American participation in the League would not serve the highest purpose of the prevention of war and a settlement of international difficulties in accordance with fundamental American ideals. Because of these facts, therefore, I do not favor American participation.[30]

In an editorial in the *New York American,* one of the Hearst newspapers, on January 16, 1935, it is stated that this speech was made in response to some correspondence between Mr. Roosevelt and Mr. Hearst in the course of which Mr. Hearst had made it perfectly clear that he would not support Mr. Roosevelt for the Presidency unless he would come out in a public statement against American membership in the League. In the same editorial it is stated that following Governor Roosevelt's address, from which the quotation is given above, Mr. Hearst supported Mr. Roosevelt and was influential in securing for him his nomination and election.

In his address before the Woodrow Wilson Foundation on December 28, 1933, President Roosevelt praised the League as "a prop in the world peace structure." He noted that "to-day the United States is coöperating more openly in the fuller utilization of the League of Nations machinery than ever before." But he added: "We are not members and we do not contemplate membership. We are giving coöperation to the League in every matter which is not primarily political, and in every

[30] *New York Times,* February 3, 1932.

matter which obviously represents the views and the good of the peoples of the world as distinguished from the views and the good of political leaders, of privileged classes, or of imperialistic aims."

On June 16, 1934, the Congress passed a joint resolution giving President Roosevelt authority to accept membership in the International Labor Organization. The joint resolution provided: "That in accepting such membership the President shall assume on behalf of the United States no obligation under the covenant of the League of Nations." [31] On June 19 this resolution was approved by the President and on June 22 the International Labor Conference unanimously adopted a resolution inviting the United States to become a member. This invitation was accepted on August 20 by a letter from the American Consul at Geneva, Mr. Gilbert, to the Director of the International Labor Organization. [32]

A notable feature of this acceptance was the absence of publicity attending the passage of the joint resolution. Public opinion in the United States was scarcely aware that the action was being taken and its significance was not at all appreciated. It seems probable that the smooth passage of the resolution was due in part to the fact that membership in the International Labor Office had never been a subject of political controversy or debate and also to the influence which President Roosevelt exercised over his party majorities in both houses of Congress. The portion of the resolution referring to the League of Nations is merely indicative of the fact that official Senatorial opinion is still awake to prevent entry into the League "through the back door."

[31] Department of State *Treaty Information Bulletin* No. 57, June 30, 1934, 18.

[32] Department of State Press Release, August 20, 1934. For the history of this action see *The Origins of the International Labor Organization*, I, Introduction by James T. Shotwell (1934).

Although there has been a very great change in the official American attitude toward the League, it is believed that this change has not extended to the point of acceptance of the idea of full League membership. Further elaboration of the present possibilities is reserved for the second half of this volume.[33]

The United States and the World Court

A consideration of the American attitude toward the Permanent Court of International Justice, or "World Court" as it is commonly known in the United States, belongs in this section, not because the executive branch of the government has treated it as a question of cooperation with the League of Nations, but because the opposition to adherence has come chiefly from opponents of the League who have detected here an attempt to secure United States entry into the League "through the back door." This point may be illustrated by the fact that Senatorial and other opponents of American adherence to the Court have constantly insisted on referring to it as the "League Court," whereas most of the proponents have been equally insistent upon calling it the "World Court."

On August 15, 1921, the Secretary of State of the United States acknowledged the receipt of a certified copy of the protocol of the Court from the Secretary General of the League. On February 24, 1923, President Harding transmitted the protocol and statute to the Senate, together with a letter from Secretary of State Hughes. The President asked for the Senate's approval of American adhesion, subject to four conditions and understandings, which were set forth in Secretary Hughes's

---

[33] *Vide infra*, p. 117 f.

letter.[33a] After Mr. Harding's death, President Coolidge, on December 6, 1923, again asked the Senate to take favorable action. The platform of both the Republican and Democratic parties endorsed the Court in the fall of 1924 and on December 3 of that year President Coolidge again urged it upon the Senate, subject to an additional condition or reservation.

In the Senate, no public attention was paid to the request of President Harding until December 10, 1923, after the first message from President Coolidge. On that date Senator Lenroot of Wisconsin introduced a resolution supporting the proposal. From that time up to March 13, 1925, numerous resolutions with various conditions and reservations were introduced. The House of Representatives, on March 3, 1925, approved by 303 votes to 28 a resolution recording its "earnest desire" that the United States should adhere to the protocol. On March 13, 1925, the Senate voted to take up the question in open executive session on December 17, 1925. The debate which began on this latter date continued until January 27, 1926, when the Senate passed a resolution approving American adherence subject to five reservations.[34]

From the very first it was apparent that the political ranks divided not on a party basis but on the basis of the attitude of Senators regarding the League of Nations and their views as to whether adherence to the Court would involve the United States in the League. Although legal arguments were attempted, the objection was not based on legal grounds so much as on the belief

---

[33a] President Harding later yielded to the foes of the League to the extent of insisting that the World Court should be divorced completely from the League. This change in his attitude was made known in an address at St. Louis on June 21, 1923, about six weeks before his death.
[34] For details of the above, see Quincy Wright, "The United States and the Permanent Court of International Justice," *International Conciliation*, No. 232, September 1927.

that the proposal to adhere to the World Court typified a policy of some sort of international collaboration which the "irreconcilables" opposed. If there were any doubt as to the legal question, it ought to have been removed by the first reservation set forth in the original proposal of Secretary of State Hughes, which expressly stipulated that adherence to the Court should "not be taken to involve any legal relation on the part of the United States to the League of Nations or the assumption of any obligation by the United States under the Covenant . . ."[35]

It is not believed necessary to dwell here in detail upon the various reservations or the arguments for and against them. It is important to analyze this subject from the point of view of its reaction on American public opinion, particularly since no other issue in foreign affairs, except possibly disarmament, has engaged so much public attention over so long a period in the United States.

The type of opposition is illustrated by the substitute proposal of one Senator in 1926 who objected to the fact that the Assembly and Council of the League acted as electoral bodies for the election of judges. He proposed that two bodies, the one constituted precisely as the Council of the League is constituted and the other constituted precisely as the Assembly of the League is constituted, should be set up for the purpose of acting as electoral bodies. So long as those bodies were not known by their League titles, he apparently had no objection to the method of the election of judges. It was the same type of objection which frequently appeared in connection with League affairs when it was argued that any meeting in Geneva should be avoided by the United States because of the implication of entanglement with

[35] Text in Manley O. Hudson, *The Permanent Court of International Justice* (1934), 211.

the League, although a meeting of precisely the same persons, dealing with precisely the same subjects, if held at the Hague, for example, would be quite unobjectionable.

Apparently with the object of making it more difficult for the President to complete the adherence of the United States to the Court statute, the Senate included in its resolution of approval, a direction to the President that the consent to the Senate's reservations must be obtained from the states parties to the Court treaty, by an exchange of notes. From the American constitutional point of view, this was clearly an infringement upon the Executive's prerogatives and it would have been entirely justifiable for the President to ignore this part of the resolution. The President, however, did not take this point of view and Secretary of State Kellogg proceeded to communicate with the other states individually.

As was to be expected, the matter was considered by the Council of the League of Nations, and the position was taken that this was a matter requiring joint consideration by all the parties to this multipartite treaty. Accordingly, a conference of the signatory states was convened at Geneva in September, 1926. The United States was invited to attend but Secretary of State Kellogg sent a rather brusque refusal. He stated that the Senate reservations were perfectly clear and that he had no authority to interpret them; both statements were inaccurate.

The conference of signatories agreed on certain counter proposals which twenty-four of the states transmitted individually to the Department of State.

There was no further move in the United States, although groups in the peace movement continued to agitate for action, until Mr. Elihu Root accepted an invitation to serve as one of a committee of jurists called to consider a revision of the statute of the Court. This committee was to meet in Geneva in March, 1929. While Mr. Root was on the high seas *en route* to Geneva, Secretary of State Kellogg sent a very conciliatory message to the Secretary General, indicating that there was really very little difference of opinion between the United States and the other powers and that the difficulties could probably be ironed out without much trouble. The sending of this note was chiefly due to Mr. Root's suggestion and influence.

It is a familiar story also that the Committee of Jurists adopted a plan prepared by Mr. Root for an acceptance of the Senate reservations. This plan in its essentials had been discussed by Mr. Root with various leaders in the Senate before he left the United States. The first reactions in the United States were favorable, but soon opposition began to develop. Some of this was due to the rather complex character of the proposed protocol for American accession and even among the friends of the Court there was considerable dissension. The failure of the pro-Court advocates in the United States to agree on the exact interpretation of the Root protocol greatly weakened the subsequent efforts for ratification. Most of the proponents of adherence were not at all fearful of American adherence under the terms of the protocol but by disagreeing on their exact significance, and particularly on the question whether the 5th reservation was fully accepted, they afforded additional strength to the opponents.

Nevertheless, the peace organizations busied themselves in the spring of 1929 in an effort to persuade President Hoover to press for immediate action by the Senate. This the President was unwilling to do on the ground that it might prejudice the success of the pending

London Naval Conference and no action was taken. If President Hoover had asserted a vigorous leadership at this time, the necessary two-thirds majority in the Senate would undoubtedly have been obtained.

The second conference of signatory states which met in Geneva in September, 1929, did not serve to spur the American government to any further activity. It was not until January 21, 1931, that Mr. Root was asked to appear before the Foreign Relations Committee of the Senate in order to explain the protocol which he drafted.

From that time on, the efforts of the pro-Court proponents were sporadic. It is almost inevitably true of the peace movement in the United States, and probably in any other country, that a certain amount of novelty and drama is necessary to keep the large constituencies roused to intense activity. It is impossible to sustain such activity among the millions of church people, members of women's organizations and the like, over a long period when nothing is actually being done. Moreover, peace organizations began to devote themselves with great fervor to the support of the cause of disarmament and this necessarily distracted their attention from the World Court.

On June 1, 1932, the Senate Foreign Relations Committee reported the protocols out to the Senate but attached additional reservations which if adopted would have practically pushed back the whole proceeding to the stage at which it was after the Senate's vote in 1926. With the termination of the Seventy-second Congress, however, the protocols automatically went back to the Foreign Relations Committee.

In 1932 a move was started in the House of Representatives to avoid the difficulties of the Senate by voting an appropriation to enable the United States to contribute its share toward the expenses of the Court.[36] Under the statute, the Court was of course open to the United States in case it cared to refer a dispute to that tribunal, even though it had not ratified the protocol. Again the proponents of American adherence to the Court were divided on the wisdom of this policy and nothing came of it. In the spring of 1934 activity was renewed in the form of public hearings before the Senate Foreign Relations Committee. On March 23 a hearing was granted to the proponents of adherence and on May 16 to the opponents. The state of public opinion on this question is sufficiently indicated by the data presented at those two hearings. The proponents were able to show that in 1933 and 1934 sixteen state legislatures had passed resolutions urging American adherence. They were able to show that the American Bar Association, as well as a great number of state and local bar associations, were in favor; [37] they were able to show that a poll of the newspapers of the country revealed that a total of 1,357 daily newspapers, with a total circulation of 26,993,906, were in favor of the Court as against 265 papers, with a total circulation of 10,557,317, opposed —the opposition being largely concentrated in the papers belonging to the Hearst chain; they were able to show that 108 World Court Committees throughout the length and breadth of the United States, including in their membership many of the most prominent citizens of the country, were actively endorsing American adherence; they were able to show that the Republican and Demo-

[36] See Manley O. Hudson "The Linthicum Resolution on the World Court," *American Journal of International Law,* XXVI, 794, October, 1932.

[37] See the pamphlet published by the American Bar Association in December 1934, edited by Professor Manley O. Hudson, entitled *In re The World Court.* This pamphlet demonstrates that the bar of the United States has never been so united on a question of public policy as it has been on this matter and that no national or other bar association has adopted any resolution opposing American adherence to the Court.

cratic platforms of 1932 reiterated the stands of both parties in favor of adherence; they were able to show that the United States Chamber of Commerce had repeatedly taken a stand in favor of adherence and that similar action had been taken by a great number of state and local chambers; they were able to show that the American Federation of Labor had repeatedly endorsed adherence, as had the National Grange and local farm groups; they were able to show that there was an overwhelming and practically unanimous endorsement by various religious groups, that practically all of the leading women's organizations, with a total membership of millions of women, were in favor of adherence, and that many other scattered groups and important individuals took the same position. The opponents, on the other hand, mustered the support of that powerful organization of veterans, the American Legion, although this body in its national conventions had twice gone on record in favor of American adherence and had reversed itself without any detailed consideration or debate; they presented the views also of the Ladies Auxiliary of the American Legion, of the Daughters of the American Revolution, the Ladies of the Grand Army of the Republic, the American War Mothers, the National Woman's Party, and other small women's organizations, largely representing similar military organizations. A number of prominent citizens also expressed their individual opposition and much was made of a poll taken by the Hearst newspapers resulting in 1,344,347 signatures. It is notable that this petition was styled "League of Nations Protest," although the petition itself included opposition to both the League of Nations and the "World Court of the League of Nations." [38]

---

[38] See United States Senate, 73rd Congress, Second Session. Committee on Foreign Relations. "Hearing Relative to the Protocols concerning the

It is thus apparent that the opposition to American adherence to the Court was largely tied up with opposition to membership in the League of Nations and in many instances was supported by such irrelevant arguments as opposition to the cancelling of the war debts, opposition to the reduction of tariffs, opposition to entangling political alliances, and so forth. The organizations in which the opposition centers are largely the self-styled "patriotic" groups. The advocates of adherence include the bar, leading business men, the religious groups, and most of the university presidents and other leaders of education. It should be borne in mind that in connection with the World Court, as in regard to other international matters, the Hearst newspapers, with their huge circulation and great political influence, continue month after month and year after year a steady barrage of editorials and cartoons, whereas the great bulk of the newspapers of the country in favor of American adherence content themselves with occasional restrained editorials and news comments. The opponents of adherence to the Court had much to say regarding the amount of money expended by the peace forces in support of their pro-Court campaign but made no reference to the enormous expenditure involved in the continuous anti-Court campaign conducted by William Randolph Hearst.

The impetus gained by the hearings before the Foreign Relations Committee in the spring of 1934 was not lost. As had been the case for ten years, the President was reluctant to push this highly controversial measure, which was opposed by powerful Senators who were giving him support on certain aspects of his domestic program. The Senators in question were particularly those belonging to the so-called Progressive Republican group and included

Adherence of the United States to the Permanent Court of International Justice," Part 1, March 23, 1934, and Part 2, May 16, 1934.

Senator Hiram Johnson of California, Senator Borah of Idaho, Senator LaFollette of Wisconsin, and Senator Shipstead of Minnesota, although the last-named is a representative of the Farmer-Labor group. On January 9, 1935, the Senate Foreign Relations Committee again reported the protocols out to the Senate by a vote of 14 to 7. This time no crippling reservations were attached, the resolution merely containing an understanding which was acceptable to the administration and to the proponents of American adherence.

Debate on the protocols was begun in the Senate on January 15 and the vote was taken on January 29 showing only 52 Senators in favor of the protocols and 36 opposed; seven votes of the necessary two-thirds were lacking.

The final debate showed that the issues of League membership and European entanglements were still confused with adherence to the Court Protocols. It should be borne in mind that, while all opponents of the World Court in the United States are also opponents of the League of Nations, not all of the proponents of the Court are advocates of American membership in the League. It is interesting to observe that in the Senate debates, little emphasis was laid upon the extent to which the United States is already coöperating with the League in the Disarmament Conference, the International Labor Organization and other matters.

Many factors entered into this controversy as they did in the League of Nations issue of 1920. The Republican Senators gave little support to the Roosevelt administration; there were difficulties in the way of the Democratic strategy. The administration was at first reluctant to yield on the traditional Senatorial insistence that no case should be referred to the Court without prior action by the Senate. A final yielding on this issue perhaps came too late or was insufficient to counteract the extreme wave of nationalism. At least some Senators realized that the militant minority opposed to the Court would punish a vote for the treaty whereas the well-intentioned majority would not reward it. Many Senators who supported the administration did so only out of party loyalty and not because of any conviction that Court membership would be valuable to the United States.

Indirectly, the result of this vote is important because it registers the continued power of that irreconcilable group in the Senate which has vigorously maintained its opposition to all measures designed to enable the United States to coöperate in measures for the stabilization of peace. It revealed also the power of such a group to sway public opinion by impassioned and unscrupulous radio appeals.

The Geneva Protocol of 1924 and Other Projects

The United States government never gave serious thought to the possibility of signing the Geneva Protocol. The fact that it attracted some attention in the United States was probably due to the fact that the Protocol was closely associated with the plan submitted independently and privately by a group of Americans, including Dr. James T. Shotwell, General Tasker H. Bliss, and Mr. David Hunter Miller. One of the chief objectives of the American or Shotwell Plan and of the Protocol was to provide a test of an "aggressor." Briefly, the test suggested was the resort to war without having previously exhausted certain agreed procedures of mediation, conciliation or arbitration. In its attempt to deal with the problem of aggression, the Shotwell Plan was coupled in American thought and comment with the resolution introduced in the Senate by Senator Borah on February

13, 1923, with a view to the "outlawry" of war.[40]   Some sections of American opinion considered the Protocol to be basically designed as an amendment to the Covenant of the League for the purpose of correcting certain deficiencies believed to exist in that instrument.[41]   In its final form, the Protocol differed widely from the original Shotwell Plan and was not acceptable to that plan's proponents.   Indeed, they left Geneva when the Protocol took shape.

There was some misinterpretation of the Protocol in the American press, as was to be expected.   This was particularly evident in regard to certain Japanese amendments, which were interpreted in some quarters as being a direct effort on the part of Japan to compel the United States to submit such questions as its immigration policy to arbitration or other international adjustment and control.

The dominant objection to the plan from the American point of view was the same as that which it is believed prevented the Protocol's ratification by the great powers of Europe, namely, the fact that it gave to the Council of the League a power to render a binding decision regarding the obligation to impose sanctions.   Even up to the present time, the states of the world have not been willing to entrust this final decision to the Council or to any other body.

It is probable that the fact that the Protocol was signed during a presidential campaign, when the country was absorbed with other matters, had some bearing on the relatively small interest displayed in it.   Mr. John W. Davis, the Democratic candidate for the presidency, was advocating closer coöperation between the United States and the League but did not stand squarely for

[40] *Congressional Record*, LXIV, pt. 4, 3605.
[41] See D. H. Miller, *The Geneva Protocol*, (1925) 10-12.

immediate American membership. His attacks on the ultra-conservative attitude of the Republican administration *vis-à-vis* the League had a tendency to put the Republican candidate, Mr. Calvin Coolidge, on the defensive. The Geneva Protocol itself was not made an issue during the campaign. Newspaper comment during the latter part of September and the first part of October, 1924, did not indicate that the issue of the Geneva Protocol affected the general stand of the press. The anti-League newspapers continued their opposition to all plans emanating from Geneva and the pro-League newspapers largely contented themselves with the same attitude as that adopted by the Democratic candidate, that is, pleading for closer coöperation with the League but not coming out for acceptance of the Protocol as a separate instrument.

As for the Draft Treaty of Mutual Assistance drawn up by the League's Temporary Mixed Commission in 1923, it can not be said that it was given much consideration in the United States. The Draft Treaty was transmitted by the Secretary General to the United States government with a request for an expression of views. The American reply was dated June 16, 1924, and constituted a flat rejection. The proposals were believed to be so intimately tied in with the League system as to make the adherence of the United States "impossible." The American government noted the possibility of "partial adherence" but believed that "the conditions imposed would of necessity be of such a character as to deprive adherence of any substantial effect." [42]

Despite its progressively coöperative attitude toward the League, and its very full measure of participation in the disarmament conferences, the United States government had nothing to do with the General Act for the

[42] League of Nations Publication, official No. A.35.1924.IX, 12-14.

Pacific Settlement of International Disputes of 1928 or the General Convention to strengthen the Means of preventing War of 1930. When the United States declined to be represented on the Committee on Arbitration and Security appointed by the Eighth Assembly, the stated grounds were that the fixed policy of the United States is "to leave to the European States those matters which are peculiarly their own concern . . ." The United States government, as a non-member of the League, could not accept proposals for control by the League which might well be acceptable to League members. "Furthermore, when the broader question of collective security pacts is raised, the geographical and constitutional situation of the United States makes its position still more special . . ." The Four Power Pact was considered by the United States entirely adequate for security in the Pacific region. The United States viewed sympathetically all efforts contributing to collective security and favored the further extension of agreements for arbitration and conciliation.[43] These arguments were sufficient to dismiss the General Act and the General Convention from further consideration. If further reasons were needed, they could be found in the inability of the United States government to extend its zeal for arbitration into the realm of treaties for compulsory arbitration.[44]

[43] Statement of Mr. Hugh Wilson, November 30, 1927. Documents of the Preparatory Commission for the Disarmament Conference, C.667. M.225.1927.IX [C.P.D. 1(d)].
[44] *Vide infra,* Chapter V.

CHAPTER TWO

THE BRIAND - KELLOGG PACT

The Reception of the Pact

There is little doubt that nothing since 1919 relating to international affairs had so fired the imagination of the American people as the multipartite treaty for the renunciation of war. As is customary in the United States, this pact goes under a number of short names. It is sometimes referred to as the Pact of Paris, sometimes as the Briand-Kellogg Pact, and perhaps most often merely as the Kellogg Pact. Undoubtedly its wide appeal was largely due to the brevity and simplicity of its terms but the general slogan to "outlaw" war appealed to the strong emotional and imaginative side of American public opinion.[1]

It will be recalled that the negotiation of the Pact began with M. Briand's offer of April 6, 1927.[2] This was a suggestion, not devoid of inspiration from a private American source, for a treaty between France and the United States. The implications and potentialities of the suggestion were quite obviously not grasped at once by the American government. M. Briand's offer seemed likely

---

[1] The substance of the Pact is contained in its two short articles as follows:

"Article I. The High Contracting Parties solemnly declare in the names of their respective peoples that they condemn recourse to war for the solution of international controversies, and renounce it as an instrument of national policy in their relations with one another.

"Article II. The High Contracting Parties agree that the settlement or solution of all disputes or conflicts of whatever nature or of whatever origin they may be, which may arise among them, shall never be sought except by pacific means."

While some significance has subsequently been attached to the preamble, so far as the public consciousness is concerned these two articles were all that counted.

[2] In general on the Pact, see J. T. Shotwell, *War as an Instrument of National Policy* (1929), and D. H. Miller, *The Peace Pact of Paris* (1928).

to sink into the limbo of grandiose schemes for the peace of the world. On April 25, 1927, President Nicholas Murray Butler of Columbia University published an open letter in the *New York Times* calling attention to the significance of the suggestion. This letter undoubtedly was the snowball which began to roll down through the snowfields of American public opinion until it became an avalanche which swept aside the timorous hesitancy of the United States Department of State. It was on June 20, 1927, that an actual draft of such a bipartite pact as was proposed was transmitted through the American Ambassador to France. Still Secretary of State Kellogg was unmoved and it was not until the 28th day of December that he made reply to the suggestion, countering with the proposal that this treaty renouncing war as an instrument of national policy should be expanded to include all of the governments of the world.

Secretary Kellogg's awakening was hastened by the introduction in the Senate, on December 8, of a resolution, of which Senator Capper was the putative author. Senator Capper's proposal was that a joint resolution of Congress should declare that it was the policy of the United States to conclude treaties formally renouncing war as an "instrument of public policy" and to settle international disputes by peaceful means. Senator Capper went further, urging the acceptance of a definition of an aggressor nation, together with the withdrawal of protection from nationals who aided such an aggressor.

In the United States, Secretary Kellogg's proposal was immediately seized upon by certain groups which for some time had been agitating for the "outlawry" of war. Mr. Salmon O. Levinson of Chicago had been particularly active in this agitation, and he secured the enthusiastic support of that powerful figure in the United States Senate, Senator Borah, who for many years occupied the influential position of Chairman of the Senate Foreign Relations Committee.

As far as public opinion in general was concerned, the legal aspects of the notion of outlawing war were widely misunderstood or wholly ignored. The differences between this plan and the Briand proposal were of no consequence to those who saw only the general ideal and were impatient with the slow processes of diplomacy which were seeking to translate this ideal into an effective instrument.

The negotiations dragged on through the winter, spring, and summer, until finally on August 27, 1928, the Pact was signed at Paris. In a Memorial Day address at Gettysburg on May 30, 1928, President Coolidge had endorsed the Pact and endorsement had also been given by the Republican National Convention at Kansas City on June 14, 1928. Such political support may be traced to the stupendous activity of the peace forces which continued unabated while the treaty was before the Senate. As Congress was convening in December, 1928, President Coolidge announced that some six hundred letters endorsing the treaty were being received daily at the Department of State and about two hundred daily additional letters at the White House.[3] The reporter of the *Manchester Guardian* was impressed by the fact that "Nine leading organisations of women with an aggregate membership running into millions have been holding joint conferences in many of the forty-eight States, primarily for the purpose of considering the Kellogg Treaty. Practically all these State conferences adopted resolutions asking for ratification without reservations. Among these organisations are such important bodies as the Young Women's Christian Association, the American Association of University Women, the Na-

[3] *New York Times*, December 8, 1928.

tional Federation of Women's Clubs, the National League of Women Voters, the National Council of Jewish Women, the Women's Christian Temperance Union, and the Women's Council for Home and Foreign Missions." [4] Petitions bearing some two million signatures were laid before the Senate at this time. Never were the peace forces in the United States more unanimous and never had they rallied to their support so many citizens not always identified with their programs. The voices in opposition were small and weak indeed. The result of the vote in the Senate was not in doubt and on January 15, 1929, that body advised and consented to ratification by a vote of 85 to 1.

In other connections it has already been pointed out that there are factors influencing the attitude of the Senate which are not necessarily influential with public opinion. It is important to note the interpretations of the Pact which were before the Senate because they were undoubtedly influential in the elimination of opposition. The report of the Senate Foreign Relations Committee, which was dated January 14, 1929,[5] while not proposing any reservation or formal interpretative resolution, emphatically stated its understandings:

(1) That the Pact did not curtail or impair the right of self-defense and that each nation was free to judge for itself just what was necessary in the exercise of this right.

(2) That the United States considers the Monroe Doctrine part of its national defense and that the right of self-defense allowed by the treaty must therefore include the right to maintain the Monroe Doctrine.

(3) "That the treaty does not provide sanctions, express or implied . . . there is no obligation or commit-

[4] *Manchester Guardian*, December 10, 1928.
[5] *Congressional Record*, LXX, 1783f.

ment, express or implied . . . to engage in punitive or coercive measures. . . ."

The question of non-impairment of the right of self-defense had already been emphatically stated by Secretary Kellogg in his note of June 23, 1928, to various governments.[6]

Subsequent Interpretations and Applications of the Pact

It is not to be assumed that the American enthusiasm for the Briand-Kellogg Pact was entirely unanimous. There were many cynical voices raised to point out the legal loopholes and to assert that the Pact was nothing but the expression of a pious wish; that it was wholly lacking in definite commitments. These charges applied particularly to the renunciation of war as an instrument of national policy in Article 1 of the Pact, especially as that article was interpreted in the diplomatic correspondence as not affecting the right of self-defense. The detractors were inclined to pay less attention to Article 2, which contains the obligation to settle all disputes "by pacific means," although some asserted that the reservation of self-defense covered this article as well. However, these were the arguments of lawyers and technicians and probably public opinion on the whole was inclined to take the Pact at its face value. It is not meant to indicate by this statement that the majority of people in the United States believed that war had been effectively outlawed; there is too much shrewdness and cynicism in the American make-up to permit so trusting an acceptance.

The first opportunity to apply the Pact came in the summer of 1929, when hostilities were threatened between the Chinese and Soviet governments in Northern

[6] *Treaty for the Renunciation of War,* U. S. Department of State Publication No. 468, (1933), 56.

Manchuria. Secretary of State Stimson began to take steps in consultation with the diplomatic representatives of other powers in Washington as early as July 18, although the treaty did not take effect until July 24. He communicated with the Chinese and Soviet governments, reminding them of their pledges under the Pact and expressing the hope that there would be no resort to hostilities. Since the United States had not yet recognized the Soviet government, Secretary Stimson communicated with them through the French government.

When fighting actually broke out in November, the Department of State intensified its activities, and on December 2 a joint appeal was made by Great Britain, France, Italy, and the United States to the two governments, calling their attention to Article 2 of the Pact and expressing the hope for a cessation of hostilities. Secretary Stimson also communicated with the other nations who had ratified the treaty, asking them to send similar messages; thirty-seven governments associated themselves with the action taken or signified their approval. A solution of the controversy was achieved by the Soviet and Chinese governments,[7] but it can scarcely be maintained that this was due solely to the Kellogg Pact.

In the midst of these discussions regarding the Sino-Russian dispute came the joint statement of President Hoover and Prime Minister Ramsay MacDonald at the Rapidan in which they declared: "Both our Governments resolve to accept the Peace Pact not only as a declaration of good intentions, but as a positive obligation to direct national policy in accordance with its pledge." On March 28, 1930, former Secretary of State Kellogg, in a public address in New York City, justified the action of his suc-

[7] See R. M. Cooper, *American Consultation in World Affairs*, (1934), 86f., and H. L. Stimson, *The Pact of Paris: Three Years of Development*, Special Supplement to *Foreign Affairs*, XI, No. 1, October, 1932.

cessor in utilizing the Pact in the Sino-Russian dispute, saying: "It is not necessary that this treaty should contain provisions for consultation in the event of threatened hostility. Such consultation is inherent in the treaty. Any of the signatory powers may call the attention of belligerents to the provisions of this treaty and urge its maintenance unimpaired, as was done in the late threatened conflict between Russia and China." [8]

When in September 1931, Manchuria was again the "cradle of conflict," this time between China and Japan, the United States government took a leading part in the international efforts to settle the controversy. Although the Nine-Power Treaty of 1922 might have been utilized by the United States government, it was not at first invoked and Secretary Stimson based his action on the Briand-Kellogg Pact. It has already been noted[9] that in participating in the activities of the League of Nations the United States consul, Mr. Prentiss Gilbert, represented the United States as a co-signatory of the Pact. In his cabled instructions to Mr. Gilbert on October 16, 1931, Mr. Stimson said: "You are authorized to participate in the discussions of the Council when they relate to the possible application of the Kellogg-Briand Pact, to which treaty the United States is a party. You are expected to report the result of such discussions to the department for its determination as to possible action. If you are present at the discussion of any other aspect of the Chinese-Japanese dispute, it must be only as an observer and auditor." [10]   In the subsequent stage of the discussions, when Ambassador Dawes was playing hide-and-seek with the Council in Paris, he issued a press statement in which he said: "As a signatory of the Pact of Paris and of the so-called Nine-Power Treaty, the United

[8] *New York Times,* March 29, 1930.
[9] *Vide supra,* p. 18.
[10] *Sen. Doc.* 55, 72d Cong., p. 18.

States is deeply interested, with its fellow signatories, in seeing that the lofty purpose of those treaties is fulfilled." [11]

On January 7, 1932, Secretary Stimson dispatched his famous note to the governments of China and Japan in which he made the following statement:

> But in view of the present situation and of its own rights and obligations therein, the American Government deems it to be its duty to notify both the government of the Chinese Republic and the Imperial Japanese government that it can not admit the legality of any situation *de facto* nor does it intend to recognize any treaty or agreement entered into between those governments, or agents thereof, which may impair the treaty rights of the United States or its citizens in China, including those which relate to the sovereignty, the independence, or the territorial and administrative integrity of the Republic of China, or to the international policy relative to China, commonly known as the open-door policy; and that it does not intend to recognize any situation, treaty, or agreement which may be brought about by means contrary to the covenants and obligations of the Pact of Paris of August 27, 1928, to which treaty both China and Japan, as well as the United States, are parties. [12]

Thus the non-recognition doctrine was added to the corollaries of the Briand-Kellogg Pact. This note of Secretary Stimson's was followed by a public letter to Senator Borah under date of February 23 in which he stated that both the Kellogg Pact and the Nine-Power Treaty had been violated and invited world-wide support of his non-recognition doctrine. On March 11 there followed the resolution to the League Assembly stating that "it is incumbent upon the Members of the League of Nations not to recognise any situation, treaty or agreement which may be brought about by means contrary to

---

[11] Department of State Press Release, November 20, 1931.
[12] *Sen. Doc.* 55, 72d Cong., pp. 53-4.

the Covenant of the League of Nations or to the Pact of Paris."[13]

The non-recognition doctrine had been adumbrated long before, notably at the Pan American Conference of 1890.[14] It was a notion which had always had a strong appeal in Latin America. It was therefore natural to find it embodied in the Argentine Anti-War Pact of 1933. Article 2 of that treaty[15] declares that the contracting parties "shall recognize no territorial arrangement not obtained through pacific means, nor the validity of an occupation or acquisition of territory brought about by armed force."

In his address before the Council on Foreign Relations on August 8, 1932, Secretary Stimson summed up the developments under the Pact, asserting, as Mr. Kellogg had done, that the Pact "necessarily carries with it the implication of consultation." This consultation he considered "inevitable. Any effective invocation of the power of world opinion involves discussion and consultation." Just three days later, President Hoover, in accepting the Republican renomination, stated: "We have given leadership in transforming the Kellogg-Briand Pact from an inspired outlawry of war to an organized instrument for peaceful settlement backed by mobilized public opinion against aggression. We shall, under the spirit of that Pact, consult with other nations in times of emergency to promote world peace. We shall enter no agreements committing us to any future course of action or which call for use of force in order to preserve peace."[16]

In the same address of August 8, 1932, Secretary

---

[13] *League of Nations Official Journal, Special Supplement* No. 101, 87-8.
[14] See Cooper, *op. cit.*, 235.
[15] *Vide infra*, p. 76.
[16] *New York Times*, August 12, 1932. The Democratic party also supported the idea of consultation during this campaign.

Stimson also emphasized a point of considerable importance, which is that the Pact necessarily puts an end to the old law of neutrality. On this point he declared:

> War between nations was renounced by the signatories of the Briand-Kellogg Pact. This means that it has become illegal throughout practically the entire world. It is no longer to be the source and subject of rights. It is no longer to be the principle around which the duties, the conduct, and the rights of nations revolve. It is an illegal thing. Hereafter when two nations engage in armed conflict either one or both of them must be wrong-doers—violators of the general treaty. We no longer draw a circle about them and treat them with the punctilios of the duelist's code. Instead we denounce them as law-breakers.
>
> By that very act we have made obsolete many legal precedents and have given the legal profession the task of reëxamining many of its codes and treatises.[17]

This thesis has provoked considerable controversy in the writings of experts but its significance and consequences have not been fully appreciated by the country at large.[18]

Thus the Pact has been interpreted by the United States Government (1) as not affecting the right of self-defense—which includes preservation of the Monroe Doctrine; (2) as necessarily implying an obligation to

[17] See Stimson, *op. cit.*

[18] As examples of various points of view regarding the Pact and its interpretations, the following are cited; further references appear in the annotations to these articles: Quincy Wright, "The Meaning of the Pact of Paris," *American Journal of International Law,* XXVII, 39-61, January, 1933, and "Collective Rights and Duties for the Enforcement of Treaty Obligations," *Proceedings of the American Society of International Law* (1932), 101-119; Edwin M. Borchard, "The Multilateral Treaty for the Renunciation of War," *American Journal of International Law,* XXIII, 116-120, January, 1929; and "Realism *vs.* Evangelism," *ibid.,* XXVIII, 108-117, January, 1934; John B. Whitton, "What Follows the Pact of Paris?", *International Conciliation,* No. 276, January, 1932; John Bassett Moore, "An Appeal to Reason," *Foreign Affairs,* XI, 547-588, July, 1933; P. C. Jessup, "The Birth, Death and Reincarnation of Neutrality," *American Journal of International Law,* XXVI, 789-793, October, 1932; Manley O. Hudson, "The Budapest Resolutions of 1934 on the Briand-Kellogg Pact of Paris," *ibid.,* XXIX, 92-94, January, 1935.

consult in case of a threatened breach of the Pact; (3) as requiring support of the non-recognition doctrine; and (4) as putting an end to the traditional notions of neutral rights.[19]

[19] Compare also Chapter IV, *infra,* on "Consultation."

CHAPTER THREE

DISARMAMENT [1]

With the technical details of disarmament this study is not concerned. Disarmament, however, has an inherent aspect which is essentially political and which very definitely affects the world problem of security. If there had ever been any question about the truth of this statement, it would have been answered long since by the French government's constant insistence upon linking security and disarmament.

From the point of view of the United States, land disarmament is not a question of great importance. The standing army of the United States has never been large in comparison with the armies of Europe. Moreover, land forces are of most particular concern to immediately adjacent states. Happily, the relations between the United States and Canada are such that the question of the size of American forces does not enter into the practical situations of the present. In respect of Mexico it might be considered that even the relatively small army of the United States constituted some threat; this, unfortunately, has been true at some periods in the past. It should be noted that it is scarcely possible to make statements which will be equally applicable to the situation of the United States in respect of the world as a whole and in respect of Latin America in particular. In studying collective security one is primarily addressing oneself to the European and Asiatic problem. This statement is not intended to minimize the importance to the republics of Central and South America of plans of this character, nor is it intended to overlook the distinctive contributions

[1] The use of the word "disarmament" is so firmly fixed in the popular mind in the United States that it is employed here for convenience; the term "limitation of armament" is, of course, more accurate.

which the jurists and statesmen of those countries have made. By and large, however, this volume deals with the United States in its European and Asiatic relationships, rather than in its purely American relationships, unless the contrary is clearly expressed.

In this general picture of American interest in plans for disarmament, which is here being considered, naval and air disarmament are of preëminent importance. At the moment the question of naval disarmament is more to the fore. It is no longer necessary, however, to enter the fields of prophecy or imagination when one addresses oneself to the limitation of air armaments. They are a potential threat even to countries separated by wide areas of land or water. Mr. Baldwin's statement of July 30, 1934, "when you think of the defense of England you no longer think of the chalk cliffs of Dover; you think of the Rhine", caused at the moment some consternation but in its particular reference to aerial warfare there is no denying the truth of the statement. It may not be many years before it is alleged that the air frontiers of the United States are on the far sides of the Atlantic and Pacific Oceans. This possibility became daily more obvious to newspaper readers in 1935 who noted that passenger planes were crossing the United States from California to New York in twelve hours and that regular trans-Pacific and trans-Atlantic passenger and mail services would probably be inaugurated within the calendar year. Yet, since Part I of this volume deals with the history of the past rather than with the future, it is possible to say that aerial disarmament has played a relatively minor rôle for the United States, since no other state has yet been disturbed by fear of an American invasion from the air.

In the field of naval disarmament, the people of the United States may be excused if they display pride in the rôle played by the United States. Whatever may be the arguments against the treaties signed at the Washington Conference on the Limitation of Armament in 1922, it is fair to say that they represent the first successful step taken by the great powers in the direction of voluntary disarmament. The London conference of 1930 was a logical and political offspring of the Washington conference. No comparable steps have been taken elsewhere in the disarmament field. Moreover, it is at least popularly believed in the United States that the Washington treaties were made possible by the large sacrifices made by the United States. The United States was then economically in a position to outbuild any rival naval powers and extensive construction was under way. Secretary of State Hughes's dramatic gesture at the opening of the conference undoubtedly contributed largely to the conference's ultimate success. Nevertheless, it is probably not even yet generally realized throughout the United States how important it was to the success of the Washington conference that the issue of disarmament was solved in conjunction with a political issue of great importance. The Four-Power and Nine-Power Treaties, providing as they did for some adjustment of the situation in the Pacific and Far East, were the necessary political concomitants of the disarmament agreement.[2] Secretary Stimson, in his open letter of February 24, 1932, to Senator Borah, declared: "No one of these treaties can be disregarded without disturbing the general understanding and equilibrium which were intended to be accomplished and effected by the group of agreements arrived at in their entirety."

It is because no comparable political adjustment seemed immediately feasible, that the naval conversations at London in the winter of 1934-1935 were unsuc-

[2] *Vide infra*, Chapter IV.

cessful.[3] This inevitable link between disarmament and political adjustments is by no means well understood by the American people. This lack of appreciation is intensified by the common tendency in pamphlets and periodical publications to classify the United States' participation in the work of the disarmament conference at Geneva among instances of "non-political" American coöperation with the League. Such classification may be desirable from the point of view of politics or propaganda but it is scarcely in accord with the facts.

The calling of the Washington conference by President Harding shortly after his inauguration was unquestionably inspired largely by a desire of the Republican party to satisfy in some measure the demands of those of its supporters who favored some form of international cooperation for the stabilization of peace. One may properly read into this Republican program a desire to distract attention from the hue and cry about the League of Nations.[4] While not a member of the League, the United States was ready not only to participate in but to initiate a program for the stabilization of peace in the Pacific area, through agreements for disarmament and consultation.

Although this Washington Disarmament Conference had been convened wholly outside the League and without reference to it, the League itself, in view of Article 8 of its Covenant, necessarily had to address itself to this subject. After various tentative approaches, the Council of the League in 1925 set up a Preparatory Commission for a disarmament conference, to which the United States, Germany, Soviet Russia, and Turkey were also

---

[3] *Vide infra,* Chapter IV.
[4] In presenting to the Senate the treaties resulting from the Washington Conference, President Harding mentioned the League and its rejection by the American people, intimating that the Washington treaties constituted a substitute contribution toward world peace.

asked to send representatives. Although the United States had shown reluctance to participate officially in prior League disarmament activities,[5] other than the Traffic in Arms Conference of 1925, this attitude rapidly changed to one of increasing collaboration. The invitation to the 1926 meeting of the Preparatory Commission was accepted and an official delegation, headed by Mr. Hugh Gibson, was present at the first session of the commission, which met in Geneva on May 18 of that year. In his first statement, Mr. Gibson made it clear that the United States favored the method of direct approach to the limitation of armaments, thereby contributing to security, rather than the indirect method of first establishing security as a prelude to disarmament. Mr. Gibson also explained that the United States delegation "would necessarily abstain from participating in submitting any report to the Council of the League, although it would not object if any other members of the Preparatory Commission individually or collectively should care to do so."[6] Statements of this kind should be considered, at least in part, as designed for home consumption in the United States; we had not yet got out of the ostrich stage of our relations with the League. This cautious attitude was further illustrated by the fact that, due to the American suggestion that the Permanent Advisory Commission and the Joint Commission were so closely bound up with the League as to make difficult harmonious American coöperation with these bodies, their names were changed to Subcommission A and Subcommission B, although their composition and functioning were not altered.[7] These statements all related to formal relation-

[5] See Hubbard, *op. cit.*, 28.
[6] *Documents of the Preparatory Commission for the Disarmament Conference,* League of Nations Publication, official No. C.425.M.158.1926. IX [C.P.D.1(a)], 73.
[7] Salvador de Madariaga, *Disarmament* (1929), 155.

ships with the League and did not block efforts to reach agreement on disarmament.

Advocacy of disarmament has been one of the points on which practically all the peace forces of the United States were able to unite. It is one of the very few topics on which they found themselves in at least partial agreement with the American Legion, although within the Legion itself there was evident some measure of disagreement between the Committee on National Defense and the Committee on World Peace and Foreign Relations. Hundreds of thousands of names of American citizens are attached to the petitions urging disarmament which are tragically stacked behind glass doors in the Salle de Conversation of the new League building where the Disarmament Conference met.

Since 1926 the United States has continued its official participation in the efforts of this League body. However, in 1927 President Coolidge sought to convene a five-power naval disarmament conference at Geneva. France and Italy declined to attend but Great Britain, Japan, and the United States did meet in such a conference, which was entirely barren of results. The conference aroused considerable interest in the United States, particularly when a Senate committee investigated the activities of a Mr. Shearer who, it was then disclosed, was in Geneva during the conference in the character of lobbyist for certain American steel and shipbuilding companies.

The failure of this conference served to discourage and retard the work of the Preparatory Commission. The problem of the Preparatory Commission was an extremely complicated and difficult one since it necessarily included limitation of armaments on land, on sea, and in the air. It also had to consider at the same time various proposals for security pacts of one kind or another. With these security pacts the United States would at first have nothing to do. An illustration of this attitude is found in the American refusal to be represented on the Committee on Arbitration and Security appointed by the Eighth Assembly in the fall of 1927.

Becoming impatient with the slow progress of the League efforts, the United States in April, 1929, proposed that the naval powers again meet separately in an attempt to agree upon further limitation of naval armaments. The result was the London Naval Conference of 1930, which did achieve some further agreement between the United States, Great Britain, and Japan, although the Franco-Italian difficulties were not adjusted.

The Senate finally consented to ratification of the London Naval Treaty but not until some opposition had been overcome. This opposition was not due to any abandonment of the principle of disarmament but rather to apprehensions aroused by the discussions at the conference of a consultative pact. Despite repeated denials, the suspicion lingered that agreement had been reached only at the price of the assumption of some obligation to defend a European power *vi et armis*.[8]

Following the successful conclusion of the London conference, the League Preparatory Commission actively resumed work and succeeded in framing a Draft Convention for the World Disarmament Conference which was to be convened on February 22, 1932. The United States did not decline to participate in discussions of any of the topics considered, even those having to do with land effectives. However, it did at this time reject the principle of budgetary limitation, partly on the erroneous ground of constitutional difficulties. In response to the invitation to the Disarmament Conference of 1932, only three countries preceded the United States in sending in

[8] *Vide infra*, pp. 69-72.

an acceptance and in submitting detailed figures regarding armaments and expenditures. Moreover, in his moratorium proposal in June, 1931, President Hoover alluded to the burden of armaments as a factor contributing to the depression and expressed the hope that success in the disarmament field would contribute to the solution of the world's economic difficulties.

When the conference opened in February, 1932, the United States proposals were limited to suggestions regarding actual limitation of armaments and failed to suggest any link between disarmament and agreements for keeping the peace. This was still the attitude taken in Mr. Gibson's statement of April 11, 1932.[9] In President Hoover's instructions to the American delegation of June 22, 1932, the thesis of restriction of offensive armaments, with increased emphasis on defensive armaments, was reiterated, but reference was made to the Kellogg-Briand Pact in supporting this thesis.[10] This theme was continued in President Roosevelt's note of May 16, 1933, to the heads of the states represented at the Disarmament Conference, although in that note he also suggested a definition of aggression based on the first movement of armed forces across the frontier.

A further development came with the declaration of Mr. Norman Davis on May 22, 1933, in which it was stated that the United States government "was willing to consult the other states in case of a threat to peace with a view to averting conflict." Further, Mr. Davis stated: "In the event that the states, in conference, determine that a state has been guilty of a breach of the peace in violation of its international obligations and take measures against the violator, then, if we concur in the judgment rendered as to the responsible and guilty party,

[9] Department of State Press Release, April 16, 1932, 354-358.
[10] Ibid., June 25, 1932, 593.

we will refrain from any action tending to defeat such collective effort which these states may thus make to restore peace."[11] Mr. Davis also made clear that the United States supported squarely the proposal for a Permanent Disarmament Commission charged with the duty and authority to supervise the observance of any agreement for disarmament. It was the willingness to suggest these measures of collaboration which encouraged the conference to carry forward the consideration of the British draft convention which included a universal pledge of consultation. The United States accepted the British proposal "wholeheartedly" as a basis on which to proceed. On May 24, 1933, a revised British text of Part I, the so-called political chapter of the MacDonald Plan, was proposed by Sir John Simon. It was drafted with definite reference to Mr. Davis's statement of May 22 and contained the following provisions:

1. In the event of a breach or threat of breach of the Pact of Paris, either the Council or Assembly of the League of Nations or one of the parties to the present Convention who are not Members of the League of Nations may propose immediate consultation between the Council or Assembly and any of the said parties to the present Convention.

2. It shall be the object of such consultation, (a) in the event of a threat of a breach of the Pact to exchange views for the purpose of preserving the peace and averting a conflict; (b) in the event of a breach of the Pact to use good offices for the restoration of peace; and (c) in the event that it proves impossible thus to restore the peace, then to determine which party or parties to the dispute are to be held responsible.

3. The provisions of the above article do not in any way prejudice the rights and obligations of the members of the League, nor conflict with nor limit the powers and duties of the Assembly and Council under the Covenant.[12]

[11] Department of State Press Release, May 27, 1933, 390.
[12] *Records of the Conference for the Reduction and Limitation of Armament.* Series B. Minutes of the General Commission, II, 494. League of Nations Publication, 1933, IX, 10.

Mr. Davis responded with a statement of perhaps greater importance than that of May 22, although the earlier declaration has received more attention in the United States:

Mr. Norman Davis (United States of America) said that, although he had not had time to give full consideration to the revised text which Sir John Simon had submitted to the General Commission, his impression was that the United Kingdom delegation had done an excellent piece of work and, so far as Mr. Norman Davis could see, the machinery and the provisions for consultation were in harmony with the declaration he had made with regard to the position of the United States of America. He hoped, therefore, that this new draft might facilitate an immediate, or very early, conclusion of this part of the Conference's work. It might be helpful, however, at the present juncture for him to state how the United States Government would relate its action to this particular part of the Convention.

As the delegates were aware, the United States Government proposed to set forth its policy in the matter of consultation and neutral rights by unilateral declaration. As an illustration and without committing himself at the moment to the exact words, this declaration would be in some such form as the following—that was to say, assuming that the form which Sir John Simon had drafted was accepted by the General Commission:

"Recognising that any breach or threat of breach of the Pact of Paris (the Briand-Kellogg Pact) is a matter of concern to all the signatories thereto, the Government of the United States of America declares that, in the event of a breach or threat of breach of this Pact, it will be prepared to confer with a view to the maintenance of peace in the event that consultation for such purpose is arranged pursuant to Articles . . . and . . . of Part I of the Disarmament Convention. In the event that a decision is taken by a conference of the Powers in consultation in determining the aggressor with which, on the basis of its independent judgment, the Government of the United States agreed, the Government of the United States will undertake to refrain from any action and to withhold protection from its citizens if engaged in activities which would tend to defeat the collective effort which the States in consultation might have decided upon against the aggressor."

This declaration would be drafted in final form previous to signature of the Disarmament Convention, and would be made at the time of the United States' deposit of ratification of that Convention.[13]

It is important to note Mr. Davis's statement that the American pledge was to take the form of a unilateral declaration and was contingent upon the successful conclusion of a disarmament agreement. There can be no question that at this time, under the leadership of Mr. Davis, the United States delegation had come to realize that a disarmament agreement must necessarily be related to the "peace machinery" of the League. They had wholly abandoned the ostrich policy and had taken an active part in discussions of both disarmament and security, although there were obviously still very definite limitations on the extent to which the United States was willing to go in accepting commitments regarding its future action. In a word, we were prepared to consult in the event of a threatened breach of the peace; we were willing to consider limiting our insistence on neutral rights where collective action was being taken against a state which we joined in recognizing as the aggressor; and finally we were among the first to recognize that the Permanent Disarmament Commission on which the United States would be represented, should have wide powers in supervising the faithful observance of any disarmament agreement.

It is unnecessary to follow the vicissitudes of the conference, especially as they hinged upon the German withdrawal. The American government feared that this withdrawal might result in an attempt by other European powers to use the Disarmament Conference as an instrument for exerting pressure on Germany. To clarify its

[13] *Records of the Conference for the Reduction and Limitation of Armaments.* Series B. Minutes of the General Commission, II, 495-6. League of Nations Publication, 1933, IX, 10.

position, Mr. Davis issued a press statement on October 16, 1933:

We are in Geneva solely for disarmament purposes. While there is a possibility of successfully carrying on disarmament negotiations, we will gladly continue to do our part. We are not, however, interested in the political element or any purely European aspect of the picture. We again make it clear that we are in no way politically aligned with any European powers. Such unity of purpose as has existed has been entirely on world disarmament matters.

Whether or not conditions are favorable to continuing the present disarmament effort is now a question for Europe, not the United States, to decide. During this week there will be consultations between the capitals of Europe. We do not wish to take an active part in these, as the implications are purely political.[14]

When the General Commission of the conference reconvened, after an interval, at Geneva on May 29, 1934, Mr. Davis again summed up the position of the United States. He stated that when he made his statement of May 22, 1933, "it was our understanding that if the United States would be willing to adopt, subject to the conditions indicated, a policy that would not hamper the possible organization of European peace, it would be possible to conclude an agreement for a reduction and limitation of armaments along the lines of the draft convention then under consideration." Continuing, Mr. Davis said:

In fact, President Roosevelt has authorized me to summarize the attitude and policy of the United States as follows: We are prepared to coöperate in every practicable way in efforts to secure a general disarmament agreement and thus to help promote the general peace and progress of the world. We are furthermore willing, in connection with a general disarmament convention, to negotiate a universal pact of non-aggression and to join with other nations in conferring on international problems growing out of any treaties to which we are a party. The United States will not,

[14] Department of State Press Release, November 4, 1933, 251.

however, participate in European political negotiations and settlements and will not make any commitment whatever to use its armed forces for the settlement of any dispute anywhere. In effect, the policy of the United States is to keep out of war, but to help in every possible way to discourage war.[15]

Mr. Davis added the suggestion of President Roosevelt, as contained in his message to Congress, that we should be glad to participate in a convention for the control of the traffic in arms and munitions, which, at the moment, seemed to be the only avenue of constructive work open to the conference. He summed up the American position by stating that "we still stand ready to advance along any constructive lines." Nevertheless, the Disarmament Conference adjourned shortly without having made any substantial progress. In both the 1933 and 1934 statements, Mr. Davis was careful to emphasize that the American proposals hinged upon the conclusion of a disarmament convention. The United States expressed a willingness to make a contribution to the stabilization of peace only if the other powers were willing to stop the race in armaments. Technically, the American offer has lapsed, but it may, of course, be renewed.[15a]

Mr. Davis's reference to a convention for the control of the traffic in arms, was followed up by the American submission at Geneva on November 20, 1934, of a draft convention, which dealt with this subject in great detail.[15b] The United States thus took the initiative in a field where it had formerly been laggard. The St. Germain Convention of 1919 and the Geneva Convention of 1925 aroused little enthusiasm on the part of the American government, although it was represented at the conference which drew up the latter treaty. The United States raised many

[15] Department of State Press Release, June 2, 1934, 332.
[15a] Perhaps Secretary Hull's address of February 16, 1935, may be interpreted as constituting at least an informal renewal.
[15b] The text of the Draft Convention is published in Department of State Press Release, December 22, 1934.

objections, constitutional and technical, to both these treaties and did not press for their ratification. The shift in attitude was due to a number of circumstances. An effective article revealing some of the evils of the international traffic in arms, was printed in the March, 1934, issue of *Fortune,* a magazine widely read by business men. It was immediately made the basis of a number of speeches in the House and Senate, including one by Senator Borah. It was republished again in pamphlet form and was widely quoted in editorial comments in the daily press. The resulting wave of popular interest facilitated the passage of the Nye resolution providing for a special Senate committee to investigate the munitions-makers. The rather lurid reports of the committee's hearings served to arouse the popular interest still further, thus contributing to the administration's readiness to go further along the lines of international control of this traffic. Press dispatches from Geneva indicated that the British and Italian governments opposed the American proposal on the ground that it went too far. In that case, the shoe would seem to be firmly laced on the other foot.

The next phase was the tripartite conversations at London in the late fall and winter of 1934 between the representatives of the United States, Great Britain, and Japan. In these conversations the Japanese government made clear its insistence upon the abolition of the 5-5-3 ratio established by the Washington treaties of 1922 and its insistence upon actual parity. It being found impossible to reach any agreement, the Japanese government, on December 29, 1934, gave notice of its intention to terminate the Washington treaty in accordance with its terms, on December 31, 1936. The Japanese government was quite unwilling to accept the American suggestion that equality of security rather than equality of armament should be taken as the basis of discussion since, from the Japanese point of view, the two principles necessarily went together.

It seems clear that developments in Japanese policy in the Far East, and the unwillingness of the United States and of Great Britain to recognize Japan's claim to a favored position in that area, were largely responsible for the failure to reach agreement. In the time which will elapse before the termination of the treaty, some new formula may be agreed upon but it seems clear that the evolution of such a formula cannot be unrelated to the political background. Possibly the proposal for neutralizing the Philippine Islands, as contemplated in the Philippine Independence Bill of March 24, 1934, may deserve consideration in this connection. Attention is already being called to it as a possible indication of an American intention to withdraw from the Far East to Hawaii.[16] Meanwhile the United States embarked upon its large naval program and, with questionable tact from the point of view of Japanese psychology, it permitted an announcement of projected naval manœuvers in Far Eastern waters to be made at the same moment when Japan gave notice of the denunciation of the treaty.

To summarize the American position, the interest of the United States in disarmament does not arise primarily out of any desire to see the armaments of others reduced merely to enhance domestic security, as is the case with the countries of Europe. Our interest is in a disarmament which will serve as some insurance of world peace with which all nations are vitally concerned; further, we are convinced that economic recovery would be promoted if the energy, resources and money now employed in building armaments, were put to work to restore normal economic life and international trade.

[16] See P. C. Jessup, "Philippine Independence," *American Journal of International Law*, XXIX, 83-87, *January 1935*

Conversely, with the exception of the Japanese and possibly British interest in the size of our navy, other countries have little concern with the American armament program. As a practical matter, the European countries desire our association in the work of disarmament chiefly because they feel that in this way it may be possible to secure our collaboration in the stabilization of peace. This explains why on the one hand the technical American disarmament proposals, at least since 1921, have generally found a polite but negative reception, while on the other hand, the suggestions of the American delegation at Geneva that a disarmament agreement might be linked with consultation, with our participation in supervision, and with some possible modification in our eventual attitude as a neutral, aroused the greatest interest and helped to give new life to the Disarmament Conference.

Since these American suggestions were presented to the conference in 1933, progress toward agreement has been blocked by political difficulties in Europe and as the European political tension has increased, the tendency of the United States to back away from any commitments of a political character has likewise increased. We have come to appreciate that no change in the armaments of the United States will affect in any real degree the attitude of the European powers as to the safe level for their own armaments. We have the growing conviction that the powers of Europe must first decide whether there is any basis on which they can voluntarily agree that the peace shall be maintained and armaments reduced. If such agreement becomes a possibility, then there is every reason to believe that the United States will find a method of helpful collaboration.

CHAPTER FOUR

CONSULTATION [1]

Consultation may be defined to cover all interchanges of views between governments, not excepting the normal diplomatic intercourse. As thus broadly defined, it of course presents no novelty for the United States. Consultation may also be defined so as to include particularly the conference method of conducting international affairs which are of interest to a number of governments. In this sense also it is no stranger to the government of the United States.[2] Current discussion, however, inclines to view consultation as applying particularly to an exchange of views relative to the solution of a controversy which is threatened or has already broken out, and which endangers the peace of the world. It is particularly in this sense that it will be considered in this chapter.

During the post-war period, the first obligations to consult which the United States assumed were embodied in the treaties signed at the Washington Disarmament Conference in 1922. The naval treaty, in Articles 21 and 22, contained rather innocuous provisions for consultation. Under Article 21 the contracting powers (the British Empire, France, Italy, Japan, and the United States) agree to "meet in conference with a view to the reconsideration of the provisions of the Treaty and its amendment by mutual agreement" in case any contracting power believes that the requirements of its national security have been materially affected by a change of circumstances. Under Article 22 any contracting power may, upon notice, suspend the obligations of the treaty during a war in which it may become engaged. "The remaining

[1] R. M. Cooper, *American Consultation in World Affairs* (1934), is an excellent and thoroughly documented study of this subject and has been largely used in the preparation of this chapter.
[2] *Vide supra*, p. 15.

64

contracting Powers shall, in such case, consult together with a view to agreement as to what temporary modifications, if any, should be made in the Treaty as between themselves." These provisions have not aroused any particular difficulty or disagreement.

The Four-Power Treaty regarding the Pacific insular possessions of the British Empire, France, Japan, and the United States provides as follows in its first two articles:

I

The High Contracting Parties agree as between themselves to respect their rights in relation to their insular possessions and insular dominions in the region of the Pacific Ocean.

If there should develop between any of the High Contracting Parties a controversy arising out of any Pacific question and involving their said rights which is not satisfactorily settled by diplomacy and is likely to affect the harmonious accord now happily subsisting between them, they shall invite the other High Contracting Parties to a joint conference to which the whole subject will be referred for consideration and adjustment.

II

If the said rights are threatened by the aggressive action of any other Power, the High Contracting Parties shall communicate with one another fully and frankly in order to arrive at an understanding as to the most efficient measures to be taken, jointly or separately, to meet the exigencies of the particular situation.

These articles were accompanied at the time of the signing of the treaty by a declaration which reads in part as follows:

That the controversies to which the second paragraph of Article I refers shall not be taken to embrace questions which according to principles of international law lie exclusively within the domestic jurisdiction of the respective Powers.

This declaration was included by the United States as a reservation at the time of ratification.

The Nine-Power Treaty, with reference to China, provides in Article 7:

The Contracting Powers agree that, whenever a situation arises which in the opinion of any one of them involves the application of the stipulations of the present Treaty, and renders desirable discussion of such application, there shall be full and frank communication between the Contracting Powers concerned.

It will be noted that Article I of the Four-Power Treaty contemplates "a joint conference," while its second article and the Nine-Power Treaty refer merely to "full and frank communication" which could take place through the ordinary diplomatic channels without any meeting of the powers concerned. It is the former method which is usually connoted by the current use of the term "consultation." In retrospect, it may be regretted that the Nine-Power Treaty did not create an effective procedure for joint conference. Such a step would have been a logical development of prior practice under the Open-Door policy which was reaffirmed in this treaty.

In presenting these treaties to the Senate, President Harding declared:

The four-power treaty contains no war commitment. It covenants the respect of each nation's rights in relation to its insular possessions. In case of controversy between the covenanting powers it is agreed to confer and seek adjustment, and if said rights are threatened by the aggressive action of any outside power, these friendly powers, respecting one another, are to communicate, perhaps confer, in order to understand what action may be taken, jointly or separately, to meet a menacing situation.

There is no commitment to armed force, no alliance, no written or moral obligation to join in defense, no expressed or implied commitment to arrive at any agreement except in accordance with our constitutional methods. It is easy to believe, however, that such a conference of the four powers is a moral warning that an aggressive nation, giving affront to the four great powers ready to focus world opinion on a given controversy, would be embarking on a hazardous enterprise. Frankly, Senators, if nations may not safely agree to respect each other's rights, and may not agree to confer if one party to the compact threatens trespass, or may not agree to advise if one party to the pact is threatened by an outside power, then all concerted efforts to tranquilize the world and stabilize peace must be flung to the winds. Either these treaties must have your cordial sanction, or every proclaimed desire to promote peace and prevent war becomes a hollow mockery.[3]

In proposing to the conference the draft of the Four-Power Treaty, Senator Lodge of the American delegation had emphatically stated that it contained "no provision for the use of force to carry out any of the terms of the agreement, and no military or naval sanction lurks anywhere in the background or under cover of these plain and direct clauses."[4] To make assurance doubly sure, the Senate resolution of March 24, 1922, advising and consenting to the ratification of the Four-Power Treaty, provided that the approval was given subject to the following reservation and understanding:

The United States understands that under the statement in the preamble or under the terms of this treaty there is no commitment to armed force, no alliance, no obligation to join in any defense.[5]

Of course there was no secret about the fact that this Four-Power Treaty was entered into partly, if not chiefly, for the purpose of inducing Great Britain and Japan to terminate the old Anglo-Japanese alliance. Article IV of the treaty expressly provides that upon the deposit of ratifications "the agreement between Great Britain and

[3] *Conference on the Limitation of Armament, Washington, D. C., 1921-1922*, Senate Document, No. 126, 67th Congress, 2d Session, 10-11.
[4] *Conference on the Limitation of Armament, Washington, November 12, 1921-February 6, 1922*, 162.
[5] *Congressional Record*, LXII, pt. 5, 4496.

Japan which was concluded at London on July 13, 1911, shall terminate."[6]

This first commitment of consultation assumed by the United States in the post-war period was thus definitely given as a *quid pro quo* to attain a political objective, namely, the abrogation of the Anglo-Japanese alliance. It was limited in three ways. First, it was limited geographically to insular possessions in the Pacific area. Second, it was limited in substance so as to exclude domestic questions; this undoubtedly was designed to cover the question of Japanese immigration into United States territory. Third, it was limited as to its consequences; the reiterated American explanations, reinforced by the Senate reservation, definitely excluded any implication that the obligation to consult commits the United States to take any action which it might be agreed, as a result of the consultation, was desirable. Thus, the constant zeal to retain liberty of action was expressed in this instance.

The next commitment to consult was assumed by the United States without fully realizing that any such obligation had been undertaken. The text of the Briand-Kellogg Pact does not refer to consultation but in the light of subsequent American interpretations, which no other power has been inclined to controvert, the consultative obligation is implicit in the Pact.[7] This interpretation was not precluded by the expression of views of the Senate Foreign Relations Committee but those views did definitely preclude any obligation "to engage in punitive or coercive measures."[8] This commitment, therefore, is limited as the first was limited in respect of possible action resulting from the consultation. It

[6] *United States Treaty Series*, No. 669.
[7] *Vide supra*, Chapter II.
[8] *Ibid.*

contains no restriction as to the geographical area affected. As to the subject matter of the consultation, it seems to be limited to matters arising from a breach or threatened breach of the Pact itself. As has been pointed out,[9] the consultative interpretation of the Pact has been put into practice, notably in the two cases involving Manchuria. In the first case, the consultation took the form merely of "communication," as under the Nine-Power Treaty. In the second case it varied between this character and that of "conference" as contemplated by the Four-Power Treaty.

The third stage in the assumption of commitments to consult was the stalemate of the London Naval Conference of 1930. The story is clearly told in the press release of the United States delegation on March 26, 1930:

Rumor was current last evening to the effect that the American delegation had made a change of their attitude toward consultative pacts and were willing to enter into such a pact for the purpose of saving the conference. It was authoritatively denied at the headquarters of the American delegation that any change had taken place in the attitude of the American delegation, and its attitude remains as its spokesmen gave it out several weeks ago. At that time it was made clear that America had no objection to entering a consultative pact as such; on the contrary, the United States is already a party to a number of treaties involving the obligation of consulting with other powers. It will not, however, enter into any treaty, whether consultative or otherwise, where there is danger of its obligation being misunderstood as involving a promise to render military assistance or guaranteeing protection by military force to another nation. Such a misunderstanding might arise, if the United States entered into such a treaty as a *quid pro quo* for the reduction of the naval force of another power. That danger has hitherto inhered in the present situation, where France has been demanding mutual military security as a condition of naval reduction, as appears from her

[9] *Vide supra*, pp. 41-43.

original statement of her case last December. If, however, this demand for security could be satisfied in some other way, then the danger of misunderstanding a consultative pact would be eliminated from an entirely different standpoint. In such a case the American delegation would consider the matter with an entirely open mind.[10]

This statement evoked two expressions of Senatorial opinion which are characteristic of a certain section of American opinion regarding consultative pacts. Senator Borah, the Chairman of the Foreign Relations Committee, stated:

It might be helpful, if someone in London would define a consultative pact and then place alongside of this definition a further definition of a security pact. A consultative pact is a security pact in disguise. In a security pact you state in the pact what you are going to do after you have consulted. In a consultative pact you conceal what you are going to do after you have consulted, but you will be forced by the logic of the hour to do precisely what you expressly agreed to do in the security pact.

A consultative pact in which the parties would not go forward and do whatever would be necessary to be done in accordance with the realities of the situation would be a pious fraud—and a fraud which under the exigencies of the hour would be rejected.[11]

Senator Shipstead declared:

To agree to consult is to agree to decide. To agree to decide is to agree to act. To agree to act is to agree that we are going into the next war. They call this the road to peace. That is what they called the Triple Alliance, and the Triple Entente, and the Quadruple Alliance.[12]

On the other hand, Senator Robinson, Democratic floor leader and a member of the American delegation

[10] *London Naval Conference: Speeches and Press Statements by Members of the American Delegation, January 20-April 29, 1930.* (Department of State Publication, Conference Series, No. 3), 35.
[11] *New York Times,* March 28, 1930.
[12] *Ibid.*

at London, sought to justify the attitude taken by the delegation. His views were expressed in a trans-Atlantic broadcast on April 20, 1930.[13] According to Senator Robinson,

No delegation asked the United States to participate in any security pact. The American delegation made it plain that the United States would not join any consultative pact which could by implication be regarded as giving security. The French said that a mere consultative pact would not take one ton off their navy. . . .

We took the position that fair limitation of armament is of itself a wholesome and effective measure of security, tending to promote international goodwill and pacific measures for adjustment of disputes. Where treaty relations are threatened or disturbed, consultation is a logical and probably inevitable process; but agreements for consultation, unless carefully safeguarded, entered into in advance, in the opinion of many, tend to the formation of alliances and to the assumption of responsibility for decisions, which might result in involvements which our people desire to avoid. . . .

A clause providing for consultation or mutual agreement might imply some measure of obligation of all who enter into it. Failure to bind ourselves to consult or mediate in no way impairs the right of the United States to consult and give advice and even tender good offices should the occasion justify, but we should be left free to act as the friend of both parties to a dispute or at least as impartial in all controversies which do not involve American rights or interests.

Of course these arguments against consultative pacts would have been equally applicable to the provisions in the Washington treaties of 1922. They would be equally applicable to the interpretation of the Briand-Kellogg Pact which was first advanced by Secretary Kellogg on March 28, 1930, and later reiterated by Secretary Stimson.[14] The difficulty seems to have been in this case that

---

[13] *Proceedings of the London Naval Conference of 1930, and Supplementary Documents* (1931), (Department of State Publication, Conference Series, No. 6), 285.

[14] *Vide supra*, pp. 43, 45.

comments in the press had definitely led American opinion to believe that a consultative pact inserted in the London Naval Treaty was designed to afford France the security which she demanded as the price of agreement to limit her armaments and it was plausibly assumed—as Senator Robinson admitted—that the French Government would not be satisfied with an agreement merely to talk. As a result of all this furore, no consultative pact was signed, although the naval limitation treaty did contain a provision similar to that found in the Washington naval limitation treaty, providing for conference in case one party felt obliged to suspend the operation of the treaty temporarily. The Senate, however, was still cautious and consented to ratification "with the distinct and explicit understanding that there are no secret files, documents, letters, understandings or agreements which in any way, directly or indirectly, modify, change, add to, or take away from any of the stipulations, agreements, or statements in said treaty. . . ."[15]

At this period, there was evidence in the United States of a desire to "implement" the Briand-Kellogg Pact. This may have had some influence upon the pronouncements of Secretary Stimson to the effect that consultation was already implicit in the agreement and that, therefore, no further treaty on the subject was necessary. Nevertheless, the agitation for separate consultative pacts continued. The success of the agitation is reflected in the platforms of the Republican and Democratic parties of June, 1932. The Republican party favored "enactment by Congress of a measure that will authorize our government to call or participate in an international conference in case of any threat of non-fulfillment of Article 2 of the Treaty of Paris (Kellogg-Briand Pact)."[16] The

15 *Congressional Record*, LXXIII, 378.
16 *New York Times*, June 16, 1932.

Democrats wanted the Pact of Paris "to be made effective by provisions for consultation and conference in case of threatened violation of treaties."[17]

It was in view of this unusual agreement between the two major party platforms that it was possible for Mr. Norman Davis, as the Chairman of the American delegation to the Disarmament Conference at Geneva, to make his statement of May 22, 1933.[18] In his first statement he merely announced that the United States was "willing to consult the other States in case of a threat to peace, with a view to averting conflict." This statement, however, may be taken as suggesting a willingness to make a treaty to that effect, since it was made in the course of a speech accepting the British draft convention containing an obligation to consult. Yet Mr. Davis indicated that the United States would set forth its position in a unilateral declaration of policy. Although he did not abandon the reiterated Senatorial view which opposes commitments to the use of force, his statement did propose that the United States, in case it concurred in the judgment of the other powers in determining that a state had resorted to war in violation of its treaties, should "refrain from any action tending to defeat such collective effort which these States may thus make to restore peace." This commitment, although ineffective in form, was of enormous importance since it indicated that under the specified circumstances the United States would waive insistence upon its rights as a neutral, in case the members of the League applied sanctions against a Covenant-breaking state. The revised British draft, submitted two days later, sought to register the advance in the American position as indicated by Mr. Davis, by provisions

[17] *New York Times,* June 30, 1932.
[18] For further details regarding this statement, *vide supra,* Chapter III.

definitely calling for consultation "in the event of a breach or threat of breach of the Pact of Paris." [19] It is notable that this text refers to consultation between the Council or Assembly of the League and any of the parties to the proposed disarmament convention. The British draft continued by specifying the objects of the consultation, which were (a) to exchange views, (b) to use good offices to restore peace if hostilities actually broke out, and (c) if peace could not be restored, "then to determine which party or parties to the dispute are to be held responsible." If to this be added Mr. Davis's declaration, the consequence of an agreement upon the state "to be held responsible" would be that the United States would lend the negative support of non-interference with sanctioning measures applied by the other states.

In endorsing this British draft on the same day, Mr. Davis emphasized that the United States government "proposed to set forth its policy in the matter of consultation and neutral rights by unilateral declaration." He then restated the position which he had announced on May 22. He announced that such a declaration of policy "would be drafted in final form previous to the signature of the Disarmament Convention, and would be made at the time of the United States' deposit of ratification of that convention." It would seem from this statement that the United States government did not then contemplate putting its obligation to consult in treaty form.

The newspaper comment was, as usual, divided, with the isolationist papers attacking this move toward "entangling alliances" and the more liberal papers hailing this constructive contribution to world peace.[20]

---

[19] For text, *vide supra*, Chapter III,
[20] See analysis of newspaper comment in *The Literary Digest*, June 3, 1933.

When Mr. Davis summed up the American position
at the new session of the Disarmament Conference on
May 29, 1934, he reiterated, on the authority of President Roosevelt, that the United States was willing to
consult. A close reading of his statement reveals that
it was then the policy of the United States "to coöperate
. . . to secure a general disarmament agreement";
"to negotiate a universal pact of non-aggression"; and
"to join with other nations in conferring on international
problems growing out of any treaties to which we are a
party." This phraseology seems to indicate that it was
still the intention of the United States to embody any
commitment to consult in some "unilateral declaration
of policy" rather than in a treaty. It should be noted
also that, while the declaration of May 22, 1933, referred to consultation merely in regard to violations of
the Pact of Paris, Mr. Davis's last statement indicates
a willingness to consult in regard to the breach of any
treaty to which the United States is a party. It should
further be noted that in this statement he was careful to
point out that the United States would not "participate
in European political negotiations and settlements and
will not make any commitment whatever to use its armed
forces for the settlement of any dispute anywhere."
While it would appear that consultation regarding a
situation arising from the violation of a treaty such as
the Pact of Paris would be in a very real sense a "European political negotiation," the distinction made by Mr.
Davis is sufficiently obvious in theory, although it might
not always be observable in practice.

It is necessary to repeat that the American offers were
contingent upon the conclusion of a Disarmament Convention.[21] At London, the United States refused to give

---

[21] See Department of State, *Treaty Information Bulletin*, No. 57, 7,
June 30, 1934.

a pledge of consultation as a *quid pro quo* for French disarmament; at Geneva, the United States demanded general disarmament as a *quid pro quo* for a pledge of consultation. The shift in initiative gave the United States a considerable strategic advantage. One other treaty deserves attention here. It is the Argentine Anti-War Treaty of non-aggression, signed at Rio de Janeiro October 10, 1933. The United States deposited its adherence on April 27, 1934, subject to the subsequent approval of the Senate, which was given on June 15, 1934.[21] At the end of 1934 the treaty had been ratified by thirty nations, including twenty-one American republics and Austria, Bulgaria, Czechoslovakia, Italy, Portugal, Rumania, Spain, Turkey and Yugoslavia. The first two articles of this treaty are similar to the first two articles of the Briand-Kellogg Pact. Article 3 reads as follows:

> In case of non-compliance by any state engaged in a dispute, with the obligations contained in the foregoing articles, the contracting states undertake to make every effort for the maintenance of peace. To that end they will adopt in their character as neutrals a common and solidary attitude; they will exercise the political, juridical or economic means authorized by international law; they will bring the influence of public opinion to bear but will in no case resort to intervention either diplomatic or armed; subject to the attitude that may be incumbent on them by virtue of other collective treaties to which such states are signatories.[22]

Although the word "consultation" is not used in this article, it seems perfectly clear that it would be impossible to adopt "a common and solidary attitude" without consultation. This treaty was originally designed as a purely South American contribution to peace.[23] It is

[22] Department of State Press Release, April 28, 1934, 234.
[23] See P. C. Jessup, "The Saavedra Lamas Anti-War Draft Treaty," *American Journal of International Law*, XXVII, 109-114, January, 1933, and "The Argentine Anti-War Pact," *ibid.*, XXVIII, 538-541, July, 1934.

open to signature by any country in the world; as already noted, it has been ratified by nine European governments. The consultation clearly implicit in the text of this treaty has no limitation in regard to geography or subject matter. It does contain the favorite limitation of the United States against the use of armed force and goes even further in banning diplomatic intervention. Apparently the cases in which consultation is called for are only those in which a party to the treaty resorts to war in defiance of its obligation thereunder; it apparently does not apply in cases where states not parties to the treaty engage in hostilities. Attention may be called to the fact that the "common and solidary attitude" which the parties agree to adopt is to be taken "in their character as neutrals."

Undoubtedly the most vigorous denunciation of the whole idea of entering into consultative pacts came from the learned and satiric pen of John Bassett Moore, dean of American international lawyers. In his article entitled "An Appeal to Reason," which appeared in *Foreign Affairs* for July, 1933, he asserted that the "commitment of the United States to such a 'consultative pact' as is desired at Geneva would, I believe, constitute the gravest danger to which the country has ever been exposed, a danger involving our very independence. . . . Of all conceivable devices the 'consultative pact' is the most pernicious. It operates both as an incentive and as a lure. While it encourages the co-partner to do what he might otherwise refrain from doing, it fails, by reason of its indefiniteness, to deter the co-partner's antagonist from doing what he might not otherwise attempt. . . ." Judge Moore marshals examples from history to sustain his thesis that a "consultative pact" is nothing more nor less than the old type of pre-war offensive and defensive alliance garbed in sheep's clothing.

So far as practice is concerned, attention has already

been called to the large extent to which the United States consulted with other powers in the Sino-Japanese controversy which began with the Manchurian incident of September, 1931.[24] The course of that consultation, however, was not steady and even but was marked by occasional solo flights such as Secretary Stimson's "non-recognition" note of January 7, 1932. The various independent moves of the United States in the course of this affair were not due to any unwillingness on the part of the Department of State to consult with the other powers. They were due, first, to the unreadiness of American opinion to accept full participation in the League discussions, and, second, to the occasional unwillingness of the League powers to go as far or as rapidly as the United States was willing to move.

In the field of Latin American affairs, the United States has consulted with League bodies in both the Chaco and the Leticia disputes. In both cases, however, the United States was reluctant to abandon efforts to secure a purely American solution of these problems and its participation in the League efforts was by no means complete.[25] During the stage when distinctly League bodies were dealing with the Chaco dispute, the United States held back. Yet this country was among the first governments to impose an embargo on arms shipments to both belligerents in accordance with the program adopted by the League.[26] On December 7, 1934, the United States agreed to appoint a member of the Neutral Commission which was being constituted by the League but it de-

[24] *Vide supra*, p. 18.
[25] In general on these two cases, see Cooper, *op. cit.*, Chapters IV and VI, and documents there cited.
[26] The Joint Resolution of May 28, 1934, authorized the President to establish these embargoes "if *after consultation* with the governments of other American Republics and with their coöperation, as well as that of such other governments as he may deem necessary" he found that such actions might "contribute to the reëstablishment of peace." (Italics are the author's.) *Congressional Record*, LXXVIII, pt. 9, 9432.

clined to collaborate with the League's Advisory Committee "on the ground that the functions of this committee were too closely bound up with League machinery and League efforts for the settlement of the dispute." The United States confined itself to expressing a readiness to "maintain informal contact with the members of the Advisory Committee for purposes of information." When, on January 16, the Chaco Committee of the League Assembly took the historic step of passing judgment against Paraguay, the special correspondent of the *New York Times* in Geneva could still say: "Prentiss B. Gilbert, United States Consul, followed the Chaco meeting from the corridor." [27]

In regard to the Leticia controversy, the United States again sought to promote a solution by Pan American consultation. When this effort failed to bring results and when the action of the League seemed likely to be more successful, the United States did collaborate with the League bodies. When the League Administrative Commission was appointed, it contained Colonel Arthur W. Brown of the United States army.

Particularly in the Chaco dispute, the efforts of the United States to provide a purely American settlement were probably hindered by the existence of a feeling in some Latin American quarters that this case afforded them an opportunity to assert their independence of the Monroe Doctrine. Under the Monroe Doctrine, the United States has not been wont to object to settlement of Latin American controversies by European conciliators or arbitrators. The action of the United States in finally coöperating in the efforts of the League, therefore, is by no means to be interpreted as an abandonment of the Monroe Doctrine. The cases illustrate the difficulty of collaborating in the peaceful adjustment of international

[27] *New York Times,* January 17, 1935.

disputes without entering fully and frankly into all of the discussions. The promptness with which the United States acted in imposing the embargo on Paraguay and Bolivia illustrates again the difference between American action and American advance commitments. At the present time, however, it appears that the United States Government will not be in a position to alter its embargo so as to make it apply to Paraguay alone, in accordance with the League's decision of January 16. Perhaps this indicates that consultation is quite possible without full participation in forceful measures agreed upon by other states parties to that consultation.

CHAPTER FIVE

ARBITRATION AND CONCILIATION

Arbitration

Traditionally, the United States has been one of the leading exponents of arbitration.[1] The three sets of arbitrations provided for under the Jay Treaty of 1794 between the United States and Great Britain mark the beginning of the modern system of the arbitration of international disputes.[2] From that date up through the second Hague Peace Conference of 1907, the United States was justly entitled to claim that it stood in the forefront of the nations endorsing this means of pacific settlement. In the period since 1919, however, although the United States has not gone backward, it has, comparatively speaking, stood still while other nations have forged ahead. There is a very definite reason for this shift in position. Prior to 1914 few states of the world had been willing to accept in any treaty a binding obligation to refer disputes to arbitration.[3] No great power had accepted obligations of this kind which went any further than those which had been assumed by the United States. The characteristic of the pre-war arbitration treaties was their inclusion of broad reservations such as vital interests,[4] national honor,[5] and the rights of third

[1] It may be noted that the word "arbitration" is used here to signify the binding decision of international legal controversies by judicial means. It is not used to designate a process of compromise or adjustment not based upon law. Cf. the definition of arbitration as contained in Article 37 of the 1907 Hague Convention for the Pacific Settlement of International Disputes: "International arbitration has for its object the settlement of disputes between States by judges of their own choice and on the basis of respect for law. Recourse to arbitration implies an engagement to submit in good faith to the award."

[2] John Bassett Moore, *International Adjudications,* Modern Series, (1929) I, x.

[3] See H. M. Cory, *Compulsory Arbitration of International Disputes,* (1932), Part I.

[4] Cf. C. A. Beard, *The Idea of National Interest* (1934).

[5] Cf. Leo Perla, *What Is "National Honor"?* (1918).

parties, which left it open to each state to avoid arbitration of any specific issue that might arise, on the ground that it fell within one of these undefinable reservations. The executive branch of the United States government had been willing to go further and had submitted more sweeping treaties to the United States Senate, but the Senate had refused to approve them. This type of difficulty in the conduct of the foreign relations of the United States has already been alluded to.[6] The United States had an enviable record of actual submissions to arbitration but had made little progress in the conclusion of advance agreements to submit. Of particular importance in this connection is the proviso insisted upon by the Senate and finally included in the type of arbitration treaty which is known by the name of Secretary of State Elihu Root, who concluded the first of the series. When a case for arbitration under such a treaty arose, arbitration could be resorted to only in accordance with an *ad hoc compromis* and this *compromis* must be submitted to the Senate for its advice and consent before it became binding on the United States.[7] This Senatorial attitude was inspired in large part by the fear of Senators from the Southern states that the President might submit to arbitration the liability of their states to pay their repudiated bonds.

The fact that the Senate has not so far abused this power when particular *compromis* have been proposed, does not alter the objection voiced by President Theodore Roosevelt that such a clause in an arbitration treaty is tantamount to saying that if a dispute arises, the parties will agree to arbitrate if they then desire to do so. No treaty is needed to register this obvious conclusion.

[6] *Vide supra*, p. 9.
[7] For a discussion and analysis of these questions, see P. C. Jessup, "The United States and Treaties for the Avoidance of War," *International Conciliation* No. 239, 7-24, April, 1928.

In the post-war situation in Europe the emphasis shifted. The European states sought to obtain through arbitration treaties further guarantees of security. Such security could be found only if the arbitration treaty contained an unlimited obligation to submit at least certain categories of disputes to arbitration whenever they arose. If there existed a difference of opinion between the two parties to the treaty as to whether the controversy was covered by its terms, according to a provision frequently inserted in post-war treaties, the designated tribunal could itself determine this previous question. This was the type of obligation which the Senate of the United States has consistently refused to approve. The mere probability that when an issue arises one party would be willing to arbitrate, is wholly inadequate to supply the European demand for security. The United States model of arbitration treaties is therefore not useful for the post-war European system.

The shift in the European attitude did not come all at once after the close of the war. This is clearly shown by the rejection of the compulsory jurisdiction feature of the jurists' draft of a statute for the Permanent Court of International Justice. At the present time the wide acceptance of the Optional Clause and other provisions for compulsory arbitration demonstrates that the shift has been rather complete.[8]

In the post-war period the United States has concluded only one new treaty of the Root type—with Liberia. There have been half a dozen renewals for five-year periods. Beginning with the Franco-American treaty of February 6, 1928, a new type has been adopted and has served as a model for some twenty-seven treaties.[9] It is

[8] See Cory, *op. cit.*, Part II.
[9] With the following countries: Abyssinia, Albania, Austria, Belgium, Bulgaria, China, Czechoslovakia, Denmark, Egypt, Estonia, Finland, France, Germany, Greece, Hungary, Iceland, Italy, Latvia, Lithuania,

unnecessary here to analyze minutely the terms of this new-type treaty.[10] Attention will be called only to the reservations, which are four in number.

The first reservation excludes matters "within the domestic jurisdiction of either of the High Contracting Parties." This reservation is common in post-war European treaties and may be traced to paragraph 8 of Article 15 of the Covenant.

The second reservation excludes any matter which "involves the interests of third parties." This is an old-type reservation which is still in vogue.[11] Properly interpreted, it is unobjectionable, but it is subject to abuse.

The third reservation excludes any matter which "depends upon or involves the maintenance of the traditional attitude of the United States concerning American questions, commonly described as the Monroe Doctrine." This reservation has been familiar since the First Hague Peace Conference of 1899 and is more or less taken for granted.

The fourth reservation excludes any matter which "depends upon or involves the observance of the obligations of France in accordance with the Covenant of the League of Nations." Since this reservation is purely French in origin and effect, it need not be considered in appraising the position of the United States.

The important thing about the reservations is the omission of the ancient shibboleths "vital interests" and "national honor." The former inclusion of these reservations implied that matters of great national importance could not be arbitrated. Their present exclusion implies that they can be. To this extent the United States follows the recent trend. The Monroe Doctrine, to be sure,

Luxembourg, Netherlands, Norway, Poland, Portugal, Roumania, Sweden, and Yugoslavia.
[10] See Jessup, *op. cit.*, 27-35.
[11] See, *e.g.*, Article 20 of the Locarno Arbitration Treaties.

is still excepted, as are the interests of third parties. The reservation of domestic questions may readily serve as a pretext for escape from arbitration in the absence of agreement to arbitrate the question of the controversy's arbitrability, but it has a very different psychological effect. It is based on a legal principle and not merely on policy.

In addition to the reservations, there is incorporated in Article II of the treaty the Senate's favorite stipulation that in every case the *compromis* must be submitted to that body for its advice and consent. As already suggested, this is the antithesis of a treaty for compulsory arbitration.

One other feature of this treaty is significant because it also follows the current modern trend. This is the combination in the same instrument of provisions for conciliation with those for arbitration.[12] It appeared from the text that this salutary result was accomplished at the cost of attaching the arbitral reservations to the formerly unqualified conciliation obligation of the Bryan treaties,[13] but this drafting defect was cured by an exchange of notes.[14]

The treaty was approved by the Senate on March 6, 1928, without public debate.[15] It attracted little popular attention, probably because it was not heralded as any startling innovation and because the contemporaneous negotiations leading to the conclusion of the Briand-Kellogg Pact held the center of the stage. The treaty was concluded at just that time in order to replace the

[12] Only in the treaty of February 16, 1931, with Switzerland, however, are there detailed provisions for conciliation; some of these treaties, like that with France, incorporate by reference the terms of the old Bryan treaties. Others have arbitration clauses only, although conciliation treaties were in many instances signed at the same time.

[13] *Vide infra,* p. 89.

[14] Printed with the text of the treaty in United States Treaty Series, No. 785.

[15] *Congressional Record,* LXIX, pt. 4, 4192.

old Root treaty which expired by limitation February 27, 1928, and also by way of celebrating the 150th anniversary of the original treaty of alliance between France and the United States.

The differing attitudes of the President and Senate toward arbitration treaties were again to be illustrated within a short time. In accordance with resolutions adopted at the Sixth International Conference of American States at Havana on February 18, 1928, a special inter-American conference on arbitration met in Washington on December 10, 1928. As a result of its deliberations, there was signed on January 5, 1929, a General Treaty of Inter-American Arbitration. This treaty was broadly framed, embodying, in the definition of questions recognized as suitable for arbitration, the four points contained in Article 36 of the Statute of the Permanent Court of International Justice. The excepted questions were only two—those within the domestic jurisdiction and those affecting third parties. It was provided (in Article 4) that if the parties could not agree within three months on framing a *compromis* it should be formulated by the Court.

Although the United States has been inclined to accept more obligations *vis-à-vis* the other American republics than with reference to other states of the world, the Senate promptly checked this advance in our commitments. It did not take action on the treaty until January 19, 1932, although a number of private groups, conscious of the progress which the ratification of the treaty would register, conducted a minor campaign in favor of the treaty. In its resolution of approval the Senate first reiterated its insistence that the *compromis* could not be concluded without its advice and consent "notwithstanding any provisions of the treaty to the contrary." Then it added a further "understanding", whose counterpart is found in a number of acceptances of the Optional Clause and other modern treaties but unusual in United States history: ". . . the provisions of this treaty shall not be applicable to pending international questions or controversies or to those which may arise in the future relative to acts prior to the date on which said treaty goes into effect, or to controversies arising under treaties negotiated prior to the date on which said treaty goes into effect." [16] It is unnecessary for the purposes of this summary to speculate on the specific cases which the Senators may have had in mind, although Panama was probably one of them. It may be assumed that the cases were specific since this has not been a usual reservation and it is doubtful that it was inserted merely *ex abundanti cautelâ*.

From the general, long-range point of view this second reservation is not so important as the first, which is the latest and still conclusive demonstration that the Senate insists on retaining full control and will not entrust to any court or other agency the power to decide whether or not a specific case falls within a general obligation to arbitrate. Neither President Hoover nor President Franklin D. Roosevelt chose to ratify the treaty with these "understandings." On February 19, 1934, President Roosevelt resubmitted the treaty to the Senate, with a request for reconsideration of the limitations which it had prescribed. No further action has yet been taken by the Senate.

The same states also signed on the same day a Protocol of Progressive Arbitration which takes note of the fact that reservations have been made and are likely to be made to this General Treaty of Inter-American Arbitration. It provided for the withdrawal of such reservations by notice. President Roosevelt, however, evidently

[16] *Congressional Record,* LXXV, pt. 2, 2243, 2248.

preferred to attempt to eliminate them in advance of ratification.[17]

Aside from the activity of a few interested groups, this treaty also aroused little popular interest throughout the United States. This was probably due to the rather curious indifference or complacence with which Pan American engagements of this character are accepted by the country at large. It may also have been due to the fact that the Senate action was delayed so long after the signing of the treaty—three years—that the matter had ceased to be news and no longer occupied the attention of the public in view of more dramatic international affairs which preëmpted the columns of the daily press.

No other type of general arbitral engagement has been concluded by the United States since 1919. The United States has not even embodied in many of its treaties the so-called "compromisory clause" whereby it is agreed that doubts or controversies arising out of that particular treaty shall be referred to an agreed arbitral body. Such a clause is included, however, in the so-called "liquor treaties" and is contained in some multipartite instruments to which the United States is a party.[18]

Conciliation

The important difference between treaties of arbitration and those calling for conciliation, mediation or inquiry lies in the fact that the former engagements contemplate reference to a tribunal with power to render a binding decision, whereas the latter involve merely an investigation, report, suggestion or recommendation

[17] Text of the General Treaty and of the Protocol in League of Nations *Treaty Series*, CXXX, 136-160.

[18] See Cory, *op. cit.*, 160 f. In respect of the whole subject of arbitration, reference should be made to the discussion of the United States attitude toward the Permanent Court of International Justice. *Vide supra*, p. 23 f.

which has no binding effect. It is due to this difference
that the United States has become a party to numerous
conciliation treaties which are unlimited in their scope and
devoid of reservations.

The most notable group of treaties of this type are
the so-called Bryan Peace Treaties, of which twenty-one
were negotiated in 1914, 1915, and 1916. At the time
of their original negotiation, with the World War in
progress, their significance was not appreciated and they
were widely regarded as rather an amusing vagary of
their colorful if somewhat eccentric eponym. They were
approved after heated debate in the Senate and at a session attended by only fifty Senators, not including some
of the bitterest opponents of the treaties, such as Senator
Lodge. In the vast post-war network of treaties for
pacific settlement, these Bryan treaties have widely served
as a model. Of course, the idea for these treaties had
been anticipated in the Hague plan for International
Commissions of Inquiry.

The important characteristics of these Bryan treaties
were, first, their all-inclusive scope and, second, their
provision for a "breathing spell" during which no act of
force could be resorted to pending the commission's report. "Any disputes" not settled by diplomacy or arbitration were to be referred to the Permanent Conciliation
Commission. It was contemplated that the commissioners
should be designated immediately and that vacancies
should be promptly filled. As a matter of fact the ap-
pointments were allowed to lapse and it was not until
quite recently that vigorous steps were taken by the Department of State to fill the rosters. This activity has
been sustained. It is obvious, however, that this is an
awkward procedure, involving as it does the constitution
of so many commissions. If the plan were used by every
country in its relations with every other, it would be un-

wieldy and there would not be a sufficient number of competent commissioners to fill all the positions.[18a]

Aside from the Bryan treaties, eighteen new conciliation treaties of a slightly different type have been concluded since 1919.[19] Disregarding minor changes of phraseology, it may be noted that the Commission is constituted of one national (instead of two as under the Bryan treaties) of each party and three non-nationals (instead of one). The Commission is given the new power "spontaneously by unanimous agreement" to offer its services before they are requested to act by either party.

There have been other developments also in the field of international conciliation, although these have been confined to relations with the American republics. None of these developments has aroused any great measure of popular interest, either of approval or of disapproval, probably due to the fact that they were considered more or less routine developments of the accepted Bryan policy, and for the reason already noted that they were confined to engagements with other American republics and therefore did not arouse the suspicions of those who are always on the alert to detect signs of "entangling alliances" with Europe.

The first new step was the conclusion of a multipartite treaty between the United States and the five Republics of Central America. The occasion was the meeting of the second Central American Conference at Washington in 1923. The reason stated in the preamble was a desire to "unify and recast in one single Convention" the preceding Bryan Conventions. As a matter of fact, neither Nicaragua nor Salvador had ratified Bryan treaties with

[18a] It has been estimated that over 2,000 such commissions would be required.
[19] The treaty of June 19, 1930, with Greece (United States Treaty Series No. 854) is a sample.

the United States and the "permanent" commissions were non-existent in respect of Guatemala, Honduras, and Costa Rica.

This treaty [20] distinctly marks a step backward. No permanent machinery is set up, but after the dispute arises a commission of inquiry is to be constituted from names on a permanent list. In place of the unlimited scope of the Bryan treaties, this multipartite treaty restricts the field of obligation to differences of opinion "regarding questions of fact, relative to failure to comply with the provisions of any of the treaties or conventions existing between them and which affect neither the sovereign and independent existence of any of the signatory republics, nor their honor or vital interests." This treaty was ratified within two years by all the parties except Salvador, which has never ratified.

The second step was taken on South American initiative and resulted in the conclusion of the so-called Gondra Convention at the Fifth Pan American Conference at Santiago de Chile in May, 1923. This treaty, like the Bryan treaties, reserved nothing from its scope but expressly includes "all controversies which for any cause whatsoever may arise." [21] The treaty "provides for the creation of two permanent commissions, one at Washington and one at Montevideo, Uruguay. These commissions are composed of the three American diplomatic agents longest accredited in each capital. Their function is merely to receive from any state a request for the convocation of a commission of inquiry. The commission of inquiry is to be constituted forthwith. Each state appoints a national and a non-national (from another American country) and the four choose a fifth from yet another state. There are elaborate regulations stated

[20] United States Treaty Series No. 717.
[21] Text in United States Treaty Series No. 752.

for having a fifth member appointed by the President of a neutral (American) state, if the four commissioners can not agree.

"The commission is to report within a year. The report is to contain a proposal for settlement, but is merely advisory. The parties agree that they will not 'begin mobilization or concentration of troops on the frontier of the other party, nor . . . engage in any hostile acts or preparations for hostilities from the time steps are taken to convoke the commission until six months after the report is presented. The commission may fix the status of the parties pending the report, and after being convoked may make their investigation even if one state fails to appear.

"While this treaty follows closely the Bryan plan, the striking fact is that under its provisions the United States has consented to bestow upon Latin Americans a determining voice in any dispute which it may have with them. Thus if we submitted to one of these commissions a dispute with, say, Brazil, there would be four voices expressive of Latin American views and one for the United States. But the report is merely advisory, not binding. Under the Bryan treaties there would be one citizen of the United States and probably at least two Europeans. While this treaty requires the *ad hoc* creation of a commission of inquiry, the objection raised against the Central American Treaty is not pertinent because the resort by one party to the permanent commission which convokes the Commission of Inquiry operates as an immediate stay upon the hostile activities of the parties." [22]

Since this treaty is open to ratification by all American republics, it would seem to supersede and make unnecessary the Central American treaty of the same year. It might have been expected that such a treaty would be

[22] Jessup, *op. cit.*, 26-27.

most acceptable to the Latin American states, but by 1927 only the United States,[23] Brazil, Chile, Cuba, Haiti, Paraguay, and Venezuela had ratified it. Since 1928, eight other states have ratified and four more have adhered.

This treaty was in turn supplemented by the Convention of Inter-American Conciliation, signed at Washington January 5, 1929, along with the General Treaty of Inter-American Arbitration.[24] The Gondra Convention contemplated only commissions of inquiry; the 1929 treaty empowers the same commissions to act as commissions of conciliation. Moreover, the permanent commissions established under the Gondra treaty are required to act "either on their own motion when it appears that there is a prospect of disturbance of peaceful relations, or at the request of a party to the dispute." This treaty also was approved by the Senate of the United States without reservations on February 20, 1929.[25]

These provisions create for problems of the Western Hemisphere a permanent body with functions akin to some of those of the Council of the League of Nations. Their findings, however, are purely advisory and there is no obligation to comply with their recommendations.

To make more permanent the machinery set up under these treaties, an Additional Protocol to the General Convention of Inter-American Conciliation was signed at the Seventh International Conference of American States at Montevideo, December 26, 1933. The provisions of this protocol have to do with the naming of lists of persons to serve on the various commissions. The protocol con-

[23] Approved by the Senate of the United States without reservation March 18, 1924; *Congressional Record,* LXV pt. 5, 4433.
[24] United States Treaty Series No. 780.
[25] *Congressional Record,* LXX, pt. 4, 3852. Thirteen other states have also ratified.

tains no new provisions relative to the functions and jurisdiction of these bodies.[26] This protocol was approved by the Senate of the United States on June 15, 1934, and the ratification of the United States was deposited on August 18. By January 1, 1935, no other ratification had been deposited.

To this rather complicated network of conciliation treaties must be added the Argentine Anti-War Pact on non-aggression and conciliation signed at Rio de Janeiro October 10, 1933. Other articles of the treaty are referred to elsewhere in this volume[27] but attention here is concentrated on the conciliation provisions. Under Article 6, in the absence of some conciliation commission or "other international organization charged with this mission by virtue of previous treaties in effect," the parties agree to submit their differences to a conciliation commission of five members composed of one national from each country and three non-nationals. In the alternative, the task of conciliation may be entrusted to a court of justice in one of the contracting parties or to a mixed court composed of judges of courts from various countries. The report of the conciliation commission is, of course, merely advisory, and if the parties reject the solution proposed they regain their liberty of action, subject to the limitations of Articles 1 and 2 of the treaty, which require the pacific settlement of all disputes. Under Article 13, the "breathing spell" as provided in the Bryan treaties must be observed, with the parties abstaining "from any act capable of aggravating or prolonging the controversy." Article 5 suggests the possible reservations which may be made. The only two of importance as limitations upon the whole procedure of conciliation are, first, the exclusion of purely domestic questions and,

---

[26] Text in Final Act of the Conference, 185.
[27] *Vide supra,* p. 76 and *infra,* p. 117.

second, "matters which affect constitutional precepts of the parties to the controversy."

By way of summary it may be noted that the United States—due largely to the attitude of the Senate—has not since 1919 advanced toward the acceptance of compulsory arbitration. It has accepted the broadest sort of obligation in respect of inquiry and conciliation. Although there was a tendency to go further in the assumption of such obligations to other American republics, there is no reason on the basis of this history to believe that the United States Government is not now prepared to go equally far with non-American states, always provided it retains full liberty of action to accept or reject the report or recommendation. It is notable that in many cases the United States has ratified with remarkable promptness such treaties as it was willing to accept.

CHAPTER SIX

CONCLUSION

In the foregoing chapters certain facts have been stated and certain events have been described and explanations have been ventured of the reasons behind the actions of the individuals or groups concerned in the events. It is very much more difficult to go still further back and to try to analyze why Americans think and feel as they do. Some analysis of these underlying forces is made in a recent study of American foreign policy prepared by ten members of the faculty of the University of Chicago under the auspices of the Norman Wait Harris Memorial Foundation. From this study the following sentences are quoted:

> Through much of its history the United States has had a measure of geographical isolation which has minimized the danger of external attack. Its vast undeveloped West has turned public attention toward internal development rather than toward foreign policy. Its population has been recruited from different peoples whose varied ancestral attachments might cause internal dissension if foreign politics came to the front. Its constitutional system of checks and balances has made the rapid adjustment of foreign policy difficult in normal times. These conditions have given an abnormal importance both in public opinion and in official action to traditions of foreign policy formulated early in American history by the constitutional fathers, especially by Washington, Jefferson, Madison, Monroe, and the Adamses. . . .[1]

These factors undoubtedly are important. It is scarcely possible in a volume of this kind to go back through the whole range of American history in order to study the attitude of the American people in regard to foreign affairs.[2] Of course there is no such thing as an

---

[1] *An American Foreign Policy Toward International Stability*, (1934), (Public Policy Pamphlet No. 14), 1.

[2] Professor Charles A. Beard's recent book entitled *The Idea of National Interest*, (1934), is a very interesting study of this kind.

"American attitude"; there are dozens of American attitudes. To make a composite for the purpose of logical analysis serves no useful purpose, since one would be dealing with an essentially unreal thing. Three of the chief opponents of a foreign policy of the United States directed toward full coöperation with other nations in the stabilization of peace have been Senators Henry Cabot Lodge of Massachusetts, Hiram Johnson of California, and William E. Borah of Idaho. It would be foolish to attempt to explain their attitudes solely in terms of the interests of New England, the Pacific Coast and the Middle West. The attitude of Senator Lodge after 1917 was partly the result of his personal animosity to Wilson; the attitude of Senator Borah on many occasions has been largely due to his strong desire to play a lone hand; the attitude of Senator Johnson has been due partly to a personal conviction about what is good for the United States, although this conviction, happily enough for Senator Johnson, coincides with the policy of the politically powerful Hearst press. There are still large sections of the American people who have the unlearned man's respect for the printed word—"Of course it's true; I saw it in the paper." The radio is beginning to have its influence, as is indicated by some samples of the very large response to the suggestions made over the radio by a certain Father Coughlin, who is a powerful speaker and an ardent anti-internationalist.

There is nothing novel about this reminder that a great welter of forces comes into play in creating that thing which we call public opinion. It is not even a unique characteristic of the United States. It probably is true that in the United States the great distances separating one section of the country from another have a very profound influence. This is heightened by the fact that in different states—Vermont, Louisiana, Indiana,

North Dakota—the people differ tremendously in present interest and occupation and in the racial stocks from which they spring. Contrasted with the situation in England, for example, the well educated people of the United States, by and large, are poorly informed even about the affairs of their own national government. This has become much less true in the last few years, again partly due to the radio and partly due to the fact that the economic depression has so closely affected all sections of the population that they have become very much alive to what is being done in Washington to bring about an improvement. In addition, there is the real genius of President Roosevelt for appealing to and enlisting the interest and attention of the country. As indicated above,[3] there has also been a great increase in the general interest in international affairs, due largely to the activities of numerous private organizations. However, not a few visitors to the United States have been startled by the quite extraordinary ignorance of well educated American people on questions lying within the field of American foreign policy. This ignorance is not due to native inability to grasp the subject but to a great indifference to it. It may be that this attitude is in process of transformation; certainly much has been done to bring home to the American public the inevitability of American interest in world affairs. A recent example of a very influential force in that direction is the pamphlet written for the Foreign Policy Association and World Peace Foundation by Mr. Henry A. Wallace, the Secretary of Agriculture, under the title, "America Must Choose." This pamphlet enjoyed an enormous circulation and was widely quoted. In it, Secretary Wallace weighs the pros and cons of a policy of national isolation as against a policy of "world neighborhood," reaching the conclusion that the policy

[3] *Vide supra*, p. ix.

of complete isolation is neither wise nor possible for the United States.

In some sections of the American people there is undoubtedly a very strong respect for tradition. The political stump speaker still feels he is on safe ground when he invokes the authority of the fathers of the Constitution and particularly if he can quote (usually out of their context) the words of George Washington or of Abraham Lincoln. Although economic necessity has influenced many people to draw away from this devotional attachment to traditional principles such as those embodied in the Constitution, the traditional respect is not easily obliterated.

If the great mass of the American people could be interrogated for the purpose of ascertaining their stock of information on the foreign policy of the United States, the answers would probably reveal that two things immediately came to their minds. The first of these would be Washington's Farewell Address and the second would be the Monroe Doctrine. Both of them would be roughly interpreted as meaning the same thing, namely, that the United States should stay at home and mind its own business, not participating in European quarrels or difficulties and not allowing Europe to interfere in our own. A very substantial number of citizens can always be rallied to the support of these notions without regard to their historical accuracy. It is necessary to set off against this section of the American public those who have become somewhat internationally minded. Many of these persons are identified with what is loosely called the peace movement in the United States. These groups are on occasion politically powerful, as was the case in connection with the Briand-Kellogg Pact as described above.[4] They lack the fundamental element of

---

[4] *Vide supra*, p. 39.

the political effectiveness of an organized minority in that, as a whole, they do not feel so strongly about particular questions of foreign policy as to make them willing to cast their votes solely on that issue. When great numbers of the women of the country were organized in a campaign to effect the repeal of the Eighteenth Amendment, which prohibited the manufacture and sale of alcoholic liquors, they were able to induce their supporters to set this issue up as the test to be applied to every candidate for election to the federal Congress or to the state legislatures. The peace movement, including very many of the same individuals, has never been able to achieve that kind of political effectiveness. With a few exceptions, people will not vote against a candidate for the United States Senate because of his attitude toward, for example, the World Court, but will allow their vote to be affected either by general party considerations, by the comparative merits of the rival candidate, or by the stand of the candidate on some question which affects them more closely. There have been individual instances in which a Senator's stand on foreign policy has become a real issue in an election. In some of the best known instances of this sort the reason why this issue was prominent was that some locally powerful group like the Ku Klux Klan or the Hearst papers were seeking the defeat of an individual who had expressed liberal views on international subjects and who was being opposed by so-called "one hundred per cent Americans."[5] There have been many more cases in which a general party policy on foreign affairs has influenced the voters but it is very difficult in the United States to cut across party lines in regard to individual candidates solely on the ground of that

[5] *Vide supra,* p. 10, for a brief consideration of Professor Beard's thesis regarding the importance of foreign affairs as a political issue through the history of the United States.

candidate's attitude toward any question of foreign policy. There is a common belief that, with the improvement in communications throughout the world and with the increase in American tourist travel abroad, familiarity with foreign peoples and countries will bring about a change in the more or less provincial isolationism of American thought. It is true that many of these factors have increased the practical necessity for the United States to deal with international problems but the same factors have not to any great extent had the resulting effect on public opinion which was anticipated.

It would be a mistake to suppose that these aspects of isolationism and provincialism are peculiar to the United States. They exist in many other countries. Yet in European countries, geography, propinquity, history, personal recollections of wars and invasions, compulsory military service, and many other factors have made larger sections of the population more keenly conscious of the problems of foreign policy. In the United States there seems to be a trend toward a more international point of view but this trend should not be mistaken for an already complete transformation.

There are a great many people in the United States who would like to see American foreign policy framed in accordance with the dictates of generosity and humanity. As individuals, Americans are a generous and philanthropic people but the reactions of the mass do not equal the sum of all the parts. There is always a ready response in the United States to pleas for the foreign sufferers in earthquakes and floods. As individuals, the American people might not hesitate to contribute fifty cents per capita for the relief of suffering foreign peoples, but they object most strenuously, as a nation, to being taxed five cents per capita for the relief of foreign debtors. This distinction between the individual and the mass psychology is again not peculiar to the United States. It may as well be frankly realized that national policy is determined by self-interest. It is very much to the self-interest of many European states to have the American government become a member of the League of Nations. The ultimate policy of the United States will not be determined on the basis of what is good for other peoples but what is good for its own people. This is the controlling motive which actually dominates all governments. It is quite properly argued that the United States benefits from anything which contributes to the economic or political stability of the world as a whole. It is extremely rare, however, for governments to act upon the basis of such indirect and long-term returns, because public opinion, which is not so far-sighted, will not support them. Whatever may be the views of this or that section of American public opinion, the United States government will not move far in the direction of international coöperation unless and until it is convinced that such a policy offers the greatest advantages to the United States. Even if the individuals composing the government at any one time reach this conclusion, they cannot advance far unless a considerable body of opinion through the country is converted to the same point of view.[6]

---

[6] The increasing power of the forces tending to develop an informed American opinion on international affairs is notable. In 1929 the writer, as Chairman of a committee of the Fourth Conference of Teachers of International Law and Related Subjects, made an analysis of the increased attention devoted to international subjects in American colleges and universities. The report is found in the *Proceedings* of that Conference at p. 231 f. The report showed that between 1926 and 1929 the number of students registered for courses in international affairs had increased by 52%. The number of courses in international law during the same period had increased by 48%; those in international relations by 75%; and those in diplomacy by about 54%. For the activities of private organizations, see Edith E. Ware, *The Study of International Relations in the United States* (1935).

PART II

POSSIBLE AMERICAN CONTRIBUTIONS TO COLLECTIVE SECURITY

CHAPTER ONE

INTRODUCTORY

What contribution will the United States make toward Collective Security? It is difficult to answer that question without allowing one's own predilections to influence the answer. In the interest of obtaining an objective answer to this inquiry, Part I of this volume has sketched briefly the attitudes which the United States has taken during the last fifteen years. The most obvious lesson to be learned from this history is the difference between the action of the United States when an issue has arisen and the willingness of the United States to state in advance what it will do. The foreign policy of the United States during the last fifteen years may be characterized as based upon the principle of retaining liberty of action with entire freedom to form independent judgment upon facts and situations as they arise.

Note has already been taken of the general European tendency to lay stress on the conclusion of treaties by which the states bind themselves by formal promises to take certain action in future contingencies. The expectancy that such promises will be kept is, in itself, a contribution to security, in the psychological sense of a feeling of security. That these promises are not enough, however, is indicated by the tendency to reinforce them with other promises in the form of guarantees.

Except in the Caribbean area, and in pursuance of the Monroe Doctrine, the United States has never been willing to assume this type of guarantee obligation which is so familiar to European governments. Any such undertaking is immediately hailed in the United States as an "entangling alliance," which is equivalent to labelling a bottle "Poison—for external use only." On the other hand, the history of the United States during the last fifteen years indicates that, on occasion, the American government will take certain action which may prove highly effective as a contribution to the stabilization of peace. In some situations, which will be analyzed below, it is necessary to go back of the year 1919, but in general this more recent period furnishes some clue to the probabilities of the future.

In regard to the distinction between the action of the United States and the assumption of treaty obligations, it is important to note the power of the executive. For example, in line with the Davis suggestions of 1933 and 1934, the President can make a unilateral declaration of policy just as President Monroe laid down the Monroe Doctrine. He need not, for this purpose, consult the Senate. Whether or not that policy would be permanent, would depend on its inherent merits in the sense of its lasting appeal to public opinion in general and to Congressional opinion in particular. To take another example, the President, without consulting the Senate, could withhold protection from American citizens trading with a state which resorts to war in violation of treaty obligations.

Whether or not the President would take action along certain lines, would depend partly on his general policy and partly on his strength in the country. There are some things he might be willing to do and constitutionally able to do, but which, for reasons of political expediency, he might refrain from doing. Congressional resolutions or acts, authorizing certain kinds of executive action, are sometimes constitutionally necessary—as in the case of laying embargoes—and even if unnecessary, they may be politically desirable.

Although the President has rather wide powers of concluding executive agreements, treaties require the consent of the Senate, evidenced by a two-thirds vote. At the moment it is probably possible to say with some assurance what kind of treaties the Senate will accept. Until there has been further development in the Senatorial attitude, it is useless to discuss proposals going beyond this point. For instance, there is no use discussing treaties for compulsory arbitration such as the Optional Clause of the Permanent Court of International Justice. Once the foreign governments accept this premise, the question then is how much value they attribute to executive declarations of policy which are subject to alteration when a new administration takes office.

A further distinction should be made in regard to specific points which it might be inappropriate to include in a general declaration of policy and yet in regard to which the particular administration might be willing to act in a certain way. For cases of this kind also, foreign governments might be able to rely on the continuation of the policy only so long as that particular administration retained its authority.

It may well be that in regard to many matters concerning which foreign governments would like to know in advance the attitude of the United States, they will not be able to obtain even the satisfaction of an executive declaration of policy. In such cases they must gamble on something still more meager. American Presidents and Secretaries of State are on the whole cautious about making private commitments, although President Theodore Roosevelt did not hesitate on occasion to make clear what his probable line of action would be in case certain eventualities developed. The Lansing-Ishii agreement between the United States and Japan has frequently been considered to be in the nature of a secret alliance. President Wilson found that he was unable to act along lines to which he had publicly committed himself. It is probably always true that in the normal course of the routine conversations between Secretaries of State and foreign diplomatic representatives, or between American ambassadors and ministers abroad and Foreign Offices of other countries, some indication will be given regarding the probable action of the American government. Such indications are reliable only when they relate to action which the President may take on his own authority, unless he has already ascertained that the Senate will support him in measures requiring the ratification of a treaty.

Naturally, one must take into account sudden developments in public opinion which may force the President to alter his policy. The Senate's debate on the World Court in January, 1935, brought forth a series of radio talks which demonstrated the enormous power of this method of propaganda in the hands of agitators. As a medium by which an unscrupulous orator may mislead and inflame public opinion, the radio has no peer. The traditional American devotion to freedom of speech makes effective control impossible. With half-truth, innuendo or downright falsehood, the demagogue on the radio can fan that distrust of Europe which is always latent in the minds of many Americans. The listener is readily persuaded that Europeans tricked America into the World War, paid for the war with American money, took to themselves the spoils of the Peace Conference, and then repudiated their debts to America. To the thoughtless or uninformed, the conclusion seems inevitable that the United States should reject any new European proposal which is represented to him as being part of a trap to force Americans again to fight Europe's battles. Such seeds sown by the demagogue are not blighted by the calm and authoritative rebuttal of the expert, even though he also "goes on the air." In other countries as well as the United States this situation involves grave danger to world peace and order. In the United States it makes more than usually hazardous the task of forecasting probable government policy or actions. The task is essayed here with what the writer hopes is not an unfair balance of optimism and pessimism. The following pages will consider (1) some of the more general aspects of the subject of Collective Security; (2) the type of treaty obligation which the United States may be expected to assume; and (3) the action which the United States may be expected to take under certain circumstances, even though under no treaty obligation to take such action.[1]

[1] There is considerable current discussion in the United States regarding the possibility of taking action on international questions through Joint Resolutions of Congress; such resolutions require only a simple majority. Membership in the International Labor Organization was effected under authority of a Joint Resolution. Texas was annexed to the United States in 1845 by a Joint Resolution after a treaty of annexation had failed to secure the approval of the Senate; see J. B. Moore, *Digest of International Law* (1906), I, sec. 103. While this procedure affords a basis for interesting development, it has not been dealt with here in detail.

CHAPTER TWO

GENERAL ASPECTS OF COLLECTIVE SECURITY

Without hazarding a definition of collective security and without attempting an historical or philosophical examination of the concept, it is assumed that this term contemplates the elimination or restriction, by collective action or agreement, of recourse to violence on the part of any particular state for the purpose of carrying out the individual policy or will of that state.[1] So conceived, the problem of collective security is frequently considered as largely a procedural one, in the sense that it deals with the elaboration of plans for checking resort to violence. Viewed in a larger way, the basic focus of the problem should be found in the elimination of the causes which provoke the resorts to violence. The post-war period in Europe has been characterized by an emphasis on procedure at the expense of consideration of the fundamental causes of conflict. The League of Nations has devoted much more attention to the perfecting of the procedural articles of the Covenant—Articles 11 to 17—than it has to taking any effective action under Article 19, which it was hoped would provide a means of remedying situations which were inherently war-breeders. The efforts of the League to bring about economic and financial adjustments are not overlooked; they have been of great importance.

In the field of disarmament there is a difference of opinion whether armaments are in themselves a cause of friction and eventual violence. It can be admitted for the sake of argument that large armaments may

[1] A thorough and concise discussion of the scope of the subject appears in a memorandum prepared by Professor Maurice Bourquin for the Seventh Session of the International Studies Conference, 1934. (Published only in mimeographed form.)

promote a sense of *individual* security for the state possessing them. Yet this is true only when they are relatively larger than those of any prospective enemy. It would probably be readily agreed that large armaments do not contribute to a sense of collective security. In this instance at least, the senses of many individual securities do not equal a world sense of collective security. This is true because it is not possible for every state to be possessed of armaments sufficiently great to eliminate fear of neighboring armaments. If, however, agreements were generally carried out restricting mobile or offensive armaments, and if fixed defensive armaments were generally resorted to, it is conceivable that collective security could be promoted by the sum of individual securities based upon armaments.

If the very existence of armaments superior to those of a neighboring state constitutes a danger to the security of that state, it is impossible to expect that such danger will be eliminated *vis-à-vis* the United States and Latin America, since with the largest imaginable reduction in United States forces, the balance would still be overwhelmingly against any country of Latin America. It may be doubted whether this premise is necessarily true; for example, the United States is not considered a danger to the security of Canada or Brazil. Geographic factors and traditional political relations all enter into the picture. In any event, it is not practicable to consider in the immediate future the elimination of this element even if it is a danger; some other solution is necessary as, for example, non-aggression agreements, and the like.

On the other hand, any dissatisfaction with the existing naval situation as between the United States, Japan and Great Britain is within the realm of practical negotiation so far as agreements for limitation of armaments are concerned.

The difficulties in the way of eliminating the causes of conflict are of course staggering. Yet it is important to realize that there is a widespread feeling in the United States that all suggestions for American collaboration in devices for stabilizing peace emanate from sources which wish primarily to stabilize the *status quo,* and that if the United States responded to such suggestions it would become a partner in the perpetuation of injustice. There is much force in the argument that, while it is very praiseworthy to try to prevent war from breaking out, agreements along this line ought necessarily to imply that immediate steps will be taken to effect peaceful adjustments of situations for which states might otherwise seek a forcible remedy. The demand for fundamental political changes and the difficulty of obtaining them by peaceful means, constitute a great and constant threat to collective security, regardless of the geographical location of the area in question. The elimination of the danger certainly cannot be hoped for by way of satisfying all peoples with the *status quo.*[1a]

After these observations, it may seem inconsistent to devote attention here primarily to the procedural side of collective security. It is conceded that it would be more logical to begin with a consideration of the fundamental bases of conflict, but the scope of this study does not permit an examination of both angles of the problem and, for various reasons, it is the procedural aspect which has here been adopted for investigation, without suggesting that it is the more important of the two. It may suffice

[1a] The recent conversations and agreements between France and Italy and France and Great Britain, suggest some progress in attacking basic causes. It may be remarked, however, that these adjustments are being made along the lines of the European system which existed before 1914, and not through the machinery of the League. It may also be noted that these are adjustments of possible clashes of interest between the great powers and apparently have not yet extended to meet the desires of the small powers. Recent developments in Germany cannot be called "adjustments."

to refer at this point to some of these subjacent problems. Few deny that economic factors underlie much of the rivalry between states. Every government, quite naturally, seeks the material prosperity of its own people. It is widely assumed that this material prosperity may be promoted along four lines: (1) the development of a measure of self-sufficiency adequate for the estimated requirements of national defense; (2) the securing of markets for exportable goods, money, and services; (3) the securing of adequate sources of raw materials to supply domestic industries; (4) the protection of home markets. These objectives have frequently been pursued by the aid of numerous measures, some of which are commonly included within the term "economic nationalism," while others are often denounced as "imperialistic." Specifically, they include discriminatory tariffs, preferences, quotas, and other trade restrictions; control of currency, credit and foreign exchange; subsidized ocean and air lines; immigration control; spheres of influence or other forms of political control of areas which are of economic or military strategic importance.

It is not denied that certain recent and current policies of the United States in relation to tariffs, monetary standards, foreign exchange, foreign loans, and the like, have contributed to the general world condition of economic insecurity. In some instances in the past, American policy, partly animated by considerations of the advantage of national trade and commerce, have resulted in very definite threats to the independence of certain small countries in the Western Hemisphere.

It is of course a favorite theme for statesmen to declare that their country has no aggressive designs upon any other country or area; these statements are sometimes true. Entirely apart from any such official statement of policy or intention, it is believed to be accurate to say that the United States at the present time has no desire for additional territory or for the extension of its political control and influence over foreign countries. In fact, the tendency which appeared at the close of the nineteenth century seems to have run its course and there is a general feeling among the American people today, that the United States would probably be better off without any outlying possessions.[2] It is fair to add that the control of the Panama Canal remains a matter of primary national interest.

Statements currently appearing regarding the relations between Japan and the United States, sometimes give the impression that Japan's feeling of security is threatened by American naval policy. The American point of view, however, would be that the only motive animating the United States in these questions, is that of protection of its rights and interests, including the doctrine of the Open Door, against hostile action. This again leads us into one of those familiar phrases of diplomacy which are sufficiently vague to allow all manner of interpretations and applications. It does not seem fanciful to assert that any existing issues between Japan and the United States are less material than psychological in character and belong in the realm of what is known as "prestige." Foreign Minister Hirota recently stated before the Imperial Diet: "There exists no question between the two countries which is intrinsically difficult of amicable solution." [3] It would perhaps be more realistic to deny the impossibility of solution, but to admit its difficulty.

[2] Cf. the statement of the Committee on the Philippines, sponsored by the Foreign Policy Association and the World Peace Foundation: "From the strategic standpoint, the majority of the Committee regards the possession of the Philippines by the United States as a definite liability." Foreign Policy Committee Reports No. 2, January, 1934, 5. Attention may also be drawn to the American rejection of a mandate for Armenia after the close of the World War.

[3] New York Times, January 22, 1935.

Turning to the relations between the United States and the other American republics to the south, it may be said with considerable assurance that the "good neighbor" policy of the present Roosevelt administration has done much to improve these international relations. There have been many periods in the past when the United States government was animated by very much the same motives but, unfortunately, certain actions of the same government were so interpreted in Latin America as to offset the beneficial consequences of declarations of policy. The policy of the present Roosevelt administration has been made tangible and convincing by the actions taken in pursuance thereof. The notable examples are the abrogation of the Platt Amendment in the treaty with Cuba and the withdrawal of the American marines from Haiti. Further support of this policy is found in the Department of State's frigid reception of Senator Borah's recent resolution for interference in the internal affairs of Mexico.[3a]

In respect of American relations with the countries of Europe, there are no apparent political issues of great moment outstanding. Although at the present time the whole naval question is somewhat unsettled because of the denunciation of the Washington treaties and the failure of the recent tripartite conversations in London, the principle of parity between the British and American fleets is firmly accepted in the opinions of both countries, and both governments are apparently convinced of the

[3a] Mention should also be made of the Senate's consent on June 15, 1934, to the ratification of the Convention on Rights and Duties of States, which had been adopted by the Pan American Conference at Montevideo in 1933. This convention contains a clause denying the right of a state "to intervene in the internal or external affairs of another." The Senate's acceptance of this instrument, however, was accompanied by a rather sweeping reservation to the effect that the United States government would continue to pursue the policies and doctrines it was then following until there was an authoritative interpretation or definition of the terms embodied in the convention.

desirability of avoiding any irritation in their mutual relations. The question of the payment of the interallied debts is frequently brought up in the United States and remains an unsettling factor, but as an intergovernmental problem it can hardly be considered critical at the present time, despite the Johnson Act which unnecessarily contributed to the difficulties of an adjustment.

Unquestionably, the United States is in a position to make contributions to the termination of the world-wide economic depression. It is in a position to satisfy the expressed needs and desires of certain states in regard to security. It may with equal truth be pointed out that other governments are in the same position *vis-à-vis* the United States and *vis-à-vis* the rest of the world. The United States government, like any other government, will of course seek to secure as many advantages for its own people as it can in exchange for any contributions which it may make to the good of other peoples of the world. Unfortunately, the world has not yet reached the point at which governments, like certain high-minded philanthropists, make a sacrifice to bestow a blessing upon the world at large merely for the sake of doing a good deed or even as the result of a belief that any improvement in the world as a whole will ultimately react to the benefit of each individual state.

CHAPTER THREE

WHAT MIGHT THE UNITED STATES PROMISE TO DO?

Because of the general European emphasis upon a treaty structure for the stabilization of peace, it is appropriate to direct attention to the treaties which the United States might be willing to conclude in the interests of collective security. It seems useful to consider this topic with reference to certain categories of subject matter: (1) Non-aggression; (2) Disarmament; (3) Consultation; (4) Sanctions; (5) Arbitration and Conciliation.

Non-aggression Pacts

The Briand-Kellogg Pact is essentially a pact of non-aggression. War as an instrument of national policy is renounced. No dispute is to be settled by other than peaceful means. As already noted,[1] the right of self-defense, apparently including the right to maintain the Monroe Doctrine, is reserved.

The Argentine Anti-war Pact is similar but is expressly denominated a "pact of non-aggression". The first two articles of the pact read as follows:

Article 1

The High Contracting Parties solemnly declare that they condemn wars of aggression in their mutual relations or those with other states, and that the settlement of disputes and controversies shall be effected only by the pacific means established by international law.

Article 2

They declare that territorial questions between the High Contracting Parties must not be settled by resort to violence and that they shall recognize no territorial arrangement not obtained

[1] *Supra*, Part I, Chapter II, p. 40.

through pacific means, nor the validity of an occupation or acquisition of territory brought about by armed force.

Presumably, non-aggression pacts are designed to fulfill two functions: first, to assure other states that the contracting parties will not attack them; second, to lend assistance to the determination of an "aggressor" along the lines of the American or Shotwell plan of 1924.[1a] In so far as the first objective is concerned, the United States feels no particular need to obtain such promises from Europe nor does any government of Europe feel anxious to obtain them from the United States. As a problem of Latin American relations, such promises from the United States are of very great importance because they are linked to the whole delicate question of intervention. For reasons already stated, the field of United States relations with the other American republics will not be discussed here in detail.

With reference to relations between Japan and the United States, such pacts might be useful. From the standpoint of general formulas, however, it is doubtful whether much can be added to the Briand-Kellogg Pact. Particularly in the case of problems of the Pacific, the Four-Power and Nine-Power Treaties of the Washington Conference would seem to suffice. By Article I of the Four-Power Treaty, "The High Contracting Parties agree as between themselves to respect their rights in relation to their insular possessions and insular dominions in the region of the Pacific Ocean." Under Article II, they agree to communicate "If the said rights are threatened by the aggressive actions of any other Power." By Article I of the Nine-Power Treaty, the parties pledge themselves not to take aggressive steps against China.

[1a] *Per se,* a non-aggression pact would not contribute to the determination of an aggressor, if one proceeds on the basis of the test now widely approved in principle, namely, refusal to accept an armistice.

These treaties have not been denounced along with the naval treaty, although any party is free to terminate the Four-Power Treaty on a year's notice. The Argentine Anti-War Pact, to which the United States is a party, is open to the accession of Japan or any other country. It is doubtful whether the Japanese government would be inclined to accept it because of its emphasis on the non-recognition doctrine. Apparently, then, the only type of non-aggression pact which might be of general value if concluded by the United States, would be one which might contribute to the identification of an aggressor. None of the treaties just referred to, offers much assistance by way of defining an act of aggression although any of them might be used in conjunction with a treaty along the lines of the Shotwell Plan, declaring that state to be an aggressor which resorts to war in violation of a treaty obligation.

It is believed that there would be no insuperable objection in the United States to concluding a treaty defining aggression, if two consequences could be clarified. The United States would want to know who had authority to determine that the treaty had been violated. From the American point of view this is a large obstacle. The United States would not now ratify a treaty which gave to any outside organ the power to decide that the United States had resorted to war in violation of a treaty obligation, nor have the members of the League as yet been willing to yield such power and authority. Especially in view of the "self-defense" qualification of the Briand-Kellogg Pact and Mr. Kellogg's statement that each state "alone is competent to decide whether circumstances require recourse to war in self-defense",[2] such a plan as this is not likely to be adopted. The United States would

[2] Note of the United States government to governments signing Pact of Paris, June 23, 1928.

also want to know the consequences of such an identification of the aggressor. If the treaty expressly or by implication provided for forcible or economic sanctions, the United States would not now be willing to accept it. If progress is to be made along this line, the treaty must provide an automatic test of aggression. In his circular communication to the heads of states on May 16, 1933, President Roosevelt suggested: "That all the nations of the world should enter into a solemn and definite pact of non-aggression: That they should solemnly reaffirm the obligations they have assumed to limit and reduce their armaments, and, provided these obligations are faithfully executed by all signatory powers, individually agree that they will send no armed force of whatsoever nature across their frontiers".[3]

It will be noted that this suggestion, like the Davis declarations, was predicated upon the conclusion of a disarmament convention.[3a] In the event, however, that this or some other satisfactory *quid pro quo* were adopted, the United States presumably would still be willing to enter into such a treaty. Obligations of this type would not seem to be subject to the nationalistic objection to "entangling alliances". But even a definition as precise as this fails to meet the difficulty. When an armed clash occurs between two states, both usually allege that the other made the first move. Machinery for investigation of the truth of such allegations would have to be provided. If such machinery should be agreed to (as is possible in line with American treaties regarding commissions of inquiry), there would still remain the question of a binding decision upon the basis of the report. Again the United States would probably insist upon full liberty of action to accept or reject the report. Again, also, the

[3] Department of State Press Release, May 20, 1933, 353.
[3a] The same point is reiterated in Secretary Hull's address of February 16, 1935.

European nations might be dissatisfied with American reluctance to agree to act upon the report in certain ways, even if the United States independently accepted the findings.[4] The test suggested by President Roosevelt also seems to be inapplicable to situations arising from the mobilization of naval forces in waters near another state. The language used does not seem to be designed to cover every case where a fleet moves outside its own territorial waters.

In summary, it may be assumed that, under the declarations of the Franklin Roosevelt Administration, the United States would be willing to conclude a non-aggression pact defining aggression as the movement of armed forces across the frontiers:

(a) If the other nations are able to offer a consideration in the form of a general disarmament convention or in some other manner;

(b) If the United States retains full liberty to form its own independent judgment on the facts or on a report of an investigating commission;

(c) If the pact contains no express or implied obligation to use the armed forces of the United States against the aggressor if identified.

Disarmament Conventions

It is not necessary here to restate the precise terms of disarmament conventions which the United States would accept. It is sufficient to recall certain general points.

In the matter of naval limitation, the vital question at present is the elaboration of some basis of agreement between the United States, Great Britain and Japan. Although no mutually satisfactory formula has yet been

4 *Vide infra*, p. 126.

suggested, Mr. Norman Davis, in his address before the Council on Foreign Relations on January 29, 1935, was able to say: "My hope and belief is that a solution through coöperation and common agreement can and will be ultimately found." [5] The United States has shown an entire willingness to enter into such treaties and to couple them with reasonable undertakings relative to underlying political difficulties. When these basic aspects are considered, the problem broadens into one involving all powers with possessions in the Pacific. Important is the willingness of the United States, declared by legislative enactment, to agree to an international neutralization of the Philippine Islands. Important also is the willingness of the United States to agree that a permanent international commission shall have authority to supervise the faithful execution of a disarmament convention.

In the matter of the limitation of land and air armaments, the United States still plays the rôle of a friendly spectator, quite willing to join in an agreement which may be reached by the powers directly interested. American emphasis has been placed on the elimination of weapons of offense with full development of defensive arms and fortifications. Segregation of specific weapons in their respective categories has proved to be extremely difficult.

In regard to the limitation and regulation of the traffic in arms, the United States is quite ready to conclude a convention. The 1925 conference on this subject marked the first step in American coöperation with League efforts to secure limitation of armaments. For a time, the United States government took the position that constitutional difficulties would make it impossible for the federal government to undertake to regulate production in the several states of the Union. Fortunately, this untenable

[5] *New York Times*, January 30, 1935.

legal position has now been abandoned.[6]   On June 15, 1934, the Senate consented to ratification of the 1925 Convention.[7]

On November 20, 1934, the United States proposed at Geneva a new draft convention for the regulation and control of the manufacture of and trade in arms, and the establishment of a Permanent Disarmament Commission which would have wide powers of investigation.[8]   The investigation of the traffic in arms which is being currently pursued by a committee of the United States Senate, is expected to lead to proposals for American legislation which would effectively implement within the United States a convention of this type.

Consultation

The attitude of the United States toward consultative pacts has been stated.[9]   There is not evident any tendency on the part of the American government to withdraw from its present commitments under the treaties of 1922 dealing with the Pacific, or under the Pact of Paris or the Argentine Anti-War Pact.   The Davis declarations at Geneva, however, suggest that in so far as a global convention is contemplated, the United States would be inclined to confine itself to a unilateral declaration of policy to be made contingent upon the conclusion of a disarmament convention.   The Herriot plan of November 14, 1932, which was in large part based upon Secretary Stimson's speech of the previous August 8, gave

6 See Manley O. Hudson, "The Treaty-Making Power of the United States in Connection with the Manufacture of Arms and Ammunition", *American Journal of International Law*, XXVIII, 736-39, October, 1934.

7 Department of State, *Treaty Information Bulletin*, No. 57, 3.   The reservations respecting the sovereignty of Persia, and the postponement of the operation of the Convention until certain other states have accepted it, need not be discussed here.

8 Text in Department of State Press Release, December 22, 1934, 391.

9 *Supra*, Part I, Chapter IV.

clear indication that the French government at that time would not be content with a promise to consult unless it were coupled with an undertaking to adopt measures to make effective the result of the consultation.[10] The same French attitude had made it impossible for the United States to accept a consultation pact at the London Conference of 1930. There have been indications, however, that if certain European powers would agree to sanctions in such a treaty, France would be content with a bare promise to consult from the United States.

It may be confidently asserted that the United States Senate would not at present approve a consultative pact of the type generally desired by France. Unless the European governments are prepared to conclude a convention on disarmament or on some other subject in which the United States has a strong interest, it is doubtful whether the American government will go any further along the lines of agreement to consult.

If other governments feel that it would be useful to have the United States bound by such an agreement, they must be prepared to have the pact itself clearly avoid any implication that it calls for the application, by the United States, of sanctions of any kind. It must be clear that after the consultation, the United States will retain full liberty of judgment and decision as to any action it may wish to take.

Experience in the Manchurian, Chaco and Leticia disputes, suggests the advantage of full consultation between the United States and the members of the League. Whether or not one approves this policy, it is probable that the United States will again consult when occasion arises. Such consultations could be initiated and carried on more efficiently if the technical details were arranged

[10] See R. M. Cooper, *American Consultation in World Affairs* (1934), 66.

by agreement in advance. A treaty of this type is by no means impossible of realization. There might be Senatorial opposition to a treaty which envisaged full consultation with the Council of the League but the day may have passed when it was necessary to call the rose by another name. The recent vote in the United States Senate on the World Court Protocols suggests, however, the necessity for caution. It may be that the League will desire to take a preliminary step by obviating any legal difficulty which may linger as a result of the Japanese protests in October, 1931, against permitting the United States to be represented in the Council.[11]

In its numerous conciliation treaties,[12] the United States has agreed that its representative may investigate and discuss with representatives of other powers, disputes to which the United States is a party. It would be feasible for the United States to agree to like participation with regard to disputes in which it merely had an interest. If the point could be made clear in the United States and traditional prejudices overcome, there is no reason why such a body could not be called the Council of the League instead of a Permanent Commission of Inquiry or Conciliation.

It should be noted that the type of consultation may well be determined according to the immediate objective. In some instances, consultation may serve merely as a convenient method for extending good offices or proposing mediation. Under such circumstances it may be preferable to confine the consultation to parties rather directly concerned because of geographical or other factors. In other instances, the purpose of consultation may be to rally world opinion and to achieve unanimity. For that purpose, a consultation of many or all states

---

[11] See Cooper, *op. cit.* 207.
[12] *Supra*, p. 88 f.

may be desirable. It may be suggested, therefore, that in drafting a general consultative pact it would be useful to provide for various types of consultation. It is desirable to have a definite procedure for convoking the consultative body, perhaps on the request of any party to the pact.

Sanctions

The use of the word "sanctions" as a heading for this section may be misleading. The word connotes in some quarters, the use of armed force, or at least of economic pressure. The word is used here in a broader sense to signify any pressure used for the purpose of making effective a collective decision or judgment concerning a breach or threatened breach of world peace.

The United States will not now enter into any treaty, pact, covenant, agreement or understanding, which binds it in advance to use its military, air, or naval forces as a means of bringing pressure on a state which threatens to resort to war or actually begins hostilities. There is no realistic advantage from the American standpoint in discussing such an arrangement at this time.

Further, it may be asserted that the United States is also unwilling to bind itself in advance to apply economic or financial sanctions.

There are, however, two types of sanctions which the United States might, in view of its recent policy, agree to apply.

A. *Non-recognition.* The refusal to recognize arrangements or factual situations resulting from acts of aggression, is a weapon whose potentialities are still unknown. Its recent revival in current thought is of course due to Secretary Stimson's use of it in the Sino-Japanese dispute. The complete efficacy of its invocation in that instance may be doubted.

It has frequently been argued that this doctrine may tend to prolong disturbance and instability. It is said that there may be just settlements of unjust wars, and that under such circumstances the doctrine should not be applied. There is obvious difficulty in reaching general agreement on what is just.

In the Argentine Anti-War Pact, the United States has already formally pledged itself to "recognize no territorial arrangement not obtained through pacific means, nor the validity of an occupation or acquisition of territory brought about by armed forces." This treaty, to be sure, was primarily designed for the Western Hemisphere, but nine European states are now parties to it and it is open to the accession of other powers. There is no reason to believe that the United States would be unwilling to renew this pledge in other treaties.

B. *Modified neutrality.* The subject of neutrality is to be considered in greater detail hereafter.[13] At this point, it suffices to note that the government of the United States does not now take the view that the law of neutrality has been abolished. That being the case, it is evident that the United States might insist upon the maintenance of neutral rights while other states were applying forcible sanctions. Such a situation might provoke serious controversy and possibly conflict. The existence of this possibility is frequently cited as a reason why the provisions of Article 16 of the Covenant for the application of sanctions cannot be put into practice.[14] It is therefore a matter of some consequence if the United States is willing to agree to waive its neutral rights in

[13] *Vide infra*, p. 131.
[14] Cf. the statement of Mr. Stanley Baldwin in an address at Glasgow on November 23, 1934: "Never so long as I have any responsibility in governing this country will I sanction the British Navy's being used for an armed blockade of any country in the world until I know what the United States of America is going to do." *Times* (London), November 24, 1934.

order not to hinder the application of sanctions. On this point, the best evidence is Mr. Norman Davis's declaration of May 24, 1933, in which he said: "In the event that a decision is taken by a conference of the Powers in consultation in determining the aggressor with which, on the basis of its independent judgment, the Government of the United States agreed, the Government of the United States will undertake to refrain from any action and to withhold protection from its citizens if engaged in activities which would tend to defeat the collective effort which the states in consultation might have decided upon against the aggressor." [15]

It will be noted that this position leads back to the problem of identifying an aggressor. Under this declaration, perhaps no test of aggression would be essential, the matter being left to a decision reached in consultation upon the facts as they existed.

Arbitration and Conciliation

In so far as treaties of arbitration are concerned there is no likelihood that the United States will at the present time move forward along the line of accepting compulsory arbitration. It has been noted that the United States Senate has refused to approve ratification of the World Court Protocols, even without the Optional Clause. It should be remembered, however, that the World Court is faced in the United States with the old nationalistic hostility to membership in the League of Nations. The American attitude towards treaties of arbitration should not be measured by the attitude toward the Permanent Court of International Justice.

It is true that President Franklin Roosevelt has had

---

[15] *Supra,* p. 73. Secretary Hull referred to and reaffirmed this statement of policy in his address of February 16, 1935.

an unusually strong control of his party forces in Congress. The vote on the World Court, however, shows that he is not able to count absolutely on the two-thirds majority necessary for the approval of treaties. Of course not all of the senators who voted against the World Court could be lined up against the President on other treaties which would be subject to less vehement political attack. Yet the Administration was not able in the World Court fight to stand on the elimination of the traditional Senate reservation requiring that no individual case could be submitted to the Court except under a general or special treaty. It is not to be expected that this obstacle in American arbitration treaties will be removed in the near future. The unwillingness of the United States to go as far as most other countries of the world in concluding treaties for compulsory arbitration, is not an immediate obstacle to the stabilization of peace. The attitude of the United States on this question has not deterred other countries from concluding such agreements among themselves. Nor has it given them a feeling of insecurity due to any fear of hostile American action in case of dispute.

In respect of conciliation treaties, the United States is prepared to go much further. This is because the reports of commissions of conciliation or inquiry are merely advisory and the governments are not bound to accept their recommendations. Under the recent conciliation treaties concluded by the United States, not only with the countries of Latin America, but with other countries as well, permanent commissions exist with the power of initiating inquiry regarding disputes in which the United States may be involved. It has been pointed out that under some of these treaties the United States is represented by one national as against four non-nationals. Under some of the Latin American treaties, the United States may have no representative. Logically, there is no reason why the United States should not agree to permit the Council of the League of Nations to act under certain circumstances as a permanent commission of inquiry or conciliation. Practically, as already noted, such a proposal would be likely to arouse the usual anti-League propaganda with the possible result that such a treaty would fail to secure the approval of the Senate. Again it may be suggested that this attitude of the United States does not hinder plans for the stabilization of peace. The other nations of the world have not shown any particular concern about subjecting the action of the United States itself to the machinery of the League, as under Article 17 of the Covenant. The desire has been rather to have the United States participating officially with the League bodies in investigating and making recommendations on actions of other states. This problem has already been discussed above under the heading of "Consultation."

It is clearly the continuous policy of the United States government to extend its list of bilateral arbitration and conciliation treaties. It is not averse to concluding multipartite conventions of the same character, always reserving the ultimate right of the United States to make the final decision whether a particular dispute will be referred to arbitration or whether the recommendations of a conciliation commission will be accepted.

CHAPTER FOUR

WHAT WILL THE UNITED STATES DO?

Assuming that the United States is not prepared to accept in the form of binding treaty obligations, commitments on future action comparable to those which the members of the League have assumed and are apparently willing to assume, the question remains whether, in time of crisis, the United States will act in a way which will further or retard international efforts for the preservation of peace.[1] The crucial test is provided by a situation in which the members of the League are desirous of taking action under the sanction articles of the Covenant. Anticipation that the United States may take a stand which would nullify or seriously interfere with the action of the League is frequently alleged to be one of the chief obstacles to the effective operation of the Covenant. In analyzing this situation, it seems desirable to devote attention first to the problem of neutrality.

Neutrality

The policy of neutrality is firmly imbedded in American thought and practice. The American people are inclined to regard it as a traditional American doctrine in the same category as the Monroe Doctrine. They think of it chiefly as synonymous with keeping out of war and are not much aware of the wide difference between the legal impartiality which neutrality exacts and the factual partiality which it permits. There is little realization that this policy of neutrality, which was adopted by the administration of President Washington primarily as a means of avoiding embroilment in the French Revolu-

[1] A consideration of various situations inevitably leads to suggestions for some further agreements and thus makes impossible a clear line between this chapter and the one next preceding.

tionary Wars, resulted in America's "limited war" with France in 1798, and the War of 1812 with England. This consequence of the neutrality policy was due to the struggle for the defense of neutral rights against belligerent interference.

When the World War broke out in 1914, the United States turned to its policy of neutrality as the only alternative to war. The usual conflict over neutral rights began. In 1916, President Wilson was fearful that Allied interferences with neutral American trade might lead to a definite breach with the Allies.[2] It was partly due to the fact that the German submarine policy aroused even greater opposition and anger in America, that the United States entered the war on the side of the Allies.

When the war ended, the United States did not seek to secure an agreement on neutral rights because President Wilson believed that "neutrality is no longer feasible or desirable where the peace of the world is involved and the freedom of its peoples." The continuation of the old notion of neutrality was deemed inconsistent with the theoretical bases of the League Covenant. Nevertheless, the United States did not in practice abandon the law of neutrality nor has this law been abandoned in the practice of other states of the world.[3]

During the Russo-Polish War, Germany declared her neutrality in 1920, and on August 17, 1923, the Permanent Court of International Justice discussed Germany's neutral duties without any suggestion being made that neutrality was no longer a possible status.[4]

[2] Charles Seymour, *American Diplomacy During the World War* (1934), 77 f.
[3] "So far as I am aware, not a single party to the Versailles Treaty or a single member of the League of Nations has ever taken the position that the law of neutrality is a thing of the past." John Bassett Moore, "An Appeal to Reason", *Foreign Affairs*, XI, 561, July, 1933.
[4] Publications of the Permanent Court of International Justice, Series A/B, No. 5 (A, No. 1). See especially the dissenting opinion of Judges Anzilotti and Huber, p. 35.

At the Barcelona Conference on Freedom of Transit, convened under League auspices, in 1921, there was considerable discussion regarding the applicability of the proposed convention in time of war. The final statute contains in Article 8 the following provision: "This statute does not prescribe the rights and duties of belligerents and neutrals in time of war."[5] This text was adopted after vigorous debate, in which all the delegates who participated seemed to recognize that the problems of neutral and belligerent rights were still unsolved. Mr. Van Eysinga did indeed refer to the Covenant as changing the outlook toward war, but he did not deny the legal possibility of war and of neutrality. A subcommittee proposed an article by which the conference would have requested the League to call another conference to draw up "new conventions intended to govern the rights and obligations of belligerents and neutrals in time of war." This suggestion was not accepted, partly perhaps because Sir Cecil Hurst noted that they were then too close to the war to seek to make a regulation for the future.[6]

Article 15 of the Statute on the Régime of Navigable Waterways of International Concern, drawn up at the same period, contains an identic provision.[7]

In the following year, 1922, Great Britain, Belgium, Czechoslovakia, France, Germany and Italy signed the Convention on the Elbe. In Article 49 they make provision for *"les droits et devoirs des belligérants et des neutres."*[8]

Article 6 of the Nine-Power Treaty regarding China signed at the Washington Disarmament Conference on

[5] Manley O. Hudson, *International Legislation* (1931), I, 635.
[6] See League of Nations, *Barcelona Conference, Verbatim Reports and Texts Relating to the Convention on Freedom of Transit* (1921), 104 and 147.
[7] League of Nations, *Treaty Series* VII, 51. 61.
[8] *British and Foreign State Papers,* CXVI, 598, 609.

February 6, 1922, provides: "The Contracting Powers, other than China, agree fully to respect China's rights as a neutral in time of war to which China is not a party; and China declares that when she is a neutral she will observe the obligations of a neutral."

In the next year, 1923, there was signed the Convention Relating to the Development of Hydraulic Power affecting More Than One State. Article 9 copies the terms of Article 8 of the Statute on Transit referred to above.[9] The same is true of Article 32 of the Statute annexed to the Convention on the International Régime of Railways, signed at Geneva on December 9, 1923.[10] One may also refer to the so-called "neutrality treaties" under which the parties undertake "to remain neutral" or to "observe neutrality" in certain circumstances. Such, for example, are the German-Soviet treaty of 1926, the Austrian-Czech treaty of 1921, the Yugoslav-Italian treaty of 1924, and the Lithuanian-Soviet treaty of 1926. In connection with the last-named treaty, the Lithuanian government declared that its League membership "can not encroach upon the desire of the Lithuanian people to strive for neutrality, a policy which corresponds best with her vital interests."[11] An elaborate Convention on Maritime Neutrality was adopted at the Sixth International Conference of American States in 1928, and has been ratified by Bolivia, Nicaragua, Panama and the Dominican Republic, and by the United States on February 6, 1932.[12]

The Argentine Anti-War Pact of 1933 calls for action

[9] League of Nations, *Treaty Series*, XXXVI, 77, 83.
[10] *Ibid.*, XLVII, 57, 85.
[11] See P. C. Jessup, *American Neutrality and International Police* (1928), 95-96.
[12] Department of State, *Treaty Information Bulletin,* Supplement to No. 39, p. 24, and No. 40, p. 9. The above list of examples, with some additions and corrections, is taken from the writer's remarks printed in *Proceedings of the American Society of International Law,* 1933, 139-140.

by the contracting parties, "in their character as neutrals." [13]

Attention has already been drawn to the position taken by Secretary of State Stimson, that the Briand-Kellogg Pact had so altered the legal status of war that the old system of neutrality no longer exists.[14] In this connection, attention should be called to the fact that upon the conclusion of the Pact of Paris, the French and Czechoslovak governments stated their understanding that the Pact did not conflict with "the treaties of neutrality." [15] This understanding of the two governments was accepted by Secretary of State Kellogg in his note of April 13, 1928. It should also be noted that the ratification of the Havana Convention on Maritime Neutrality was completed by the United States four years after the Briand-Kellogg Pact came into force.

The present administration apparently does not accept the thesis that neutrality has been done away with. Recent press dispatches have announced that the State, War and Navy Departments are at work upon proposals for the elaboration of a new American neutrality policy. No official announcement has yet been made regarding the nature or scope of such proposals. It nevertheless seems clear that the United States will insist upon the continuance of the existence of neutral rights.

In his statement of May, 1933, Mr. Norman Davis indicated that the United States would be willing to waive its neutral rights by withholding protection from American citizens who sought to trade with an "aggressor," if the United States concurred in the general conclusion of the members of the League that a particular state had resorted to war in violation of its treaty obligations. The

[13] *Vide supra,* p. 76.
[14] *Vide supra,* p. 46.
[15] Notes from the French Minister of Foreign Affairs, July 14, 1928 and from the Czechoslovak Minister of Foreign Affairs, July 20, 1928.

policy of the United States Government, as announced by Mr. Davis, was contingent upon the conclusion of a general disarmament convention.

It may be unnecessary here to argue further the point that neutrality is still a legal possibility under the Covenant of the League and the Briand-Kellogg Pact.[16] The brief list of illustrations of state practice since the Covenant has come into existence seems to indicate that governmental opinion shares this point of view.[17]

The question remains whether the members of the League will be willing to offer the United States some *quid pro quo* for the abandonment of neutral rights in case of universal agreement upon identifying an aggressor. Two situations may be contemplated. First, the members of the Council may not be able to reach a unanimous agreement. In this case, it would appear that League members would be free to proclaim their neutrality and the United States would support neutral rights. Second, in the course of an attempt to reach agreement upon this subject, the League may appoint a commission of investigation comparable to the Lytton Commission. Judging from the experiences in the Manchurian, Chaco, and Leticia disputes, six months or a year or more might elapse between the date of the appointment of such a commission and the date of action upon its report.[18] It would appear that neutrality would be a possible status during this interval.

No matter whether such situations are or are not theoretically desirable, they are legal and practical possibili-

[16] See Jessup in *Proceedings of the American Society of International Law, op. cit.* For other views see Quincy Wright, "The Future of Neutrality," *International Conciliation* No. 242, September 1928; Clyde Eagleton, "Neutrality and the Capper Resolution," *New York University Law Review*, VI, 346-64, May, 1920, and authorities there cited.

[17] See also P. C. Jessup, *American Neutrality and International Police* (1928), 72 f.

[18] See suggestions for the elimination of such delay, *infra*, p. 145.

ties which should be faced. It seems clear that in both of these situations, the United States would be inclined to insist upon its neutral rights.

Some agreement might be reached in regard to neutral trade during the interval which might elapse before a decision was made regarding the identification of an aggressor. It might then be provided that if the United States independently concurs in a unanimous judgment regarding the aggressor, the United States would no longer insist upon protecting the trade of its nationals with such aggressor state. The agreement could then further provide some assurance for the security of neutral trade, at least among the neutrals themselves, in case there should be a failure of agreement upon identifying the aggressor. From the point of view of the United States, it would be necessary to go still further and to provide that even if the members of the League were unanimous in their judgment but if the United States did not concur in the judgment, the United States would place a total embargo upon shipments to all belligerents but would be free to continue trade with all neutrals. For this, perhaps, it would be useful to have a global agreement that states participating up to a certain extent in the imposition of sanctions but not full parties to the conflict, could be considered as "neutrals." Under the law of neutrality as it now exists, it might be illegal for the United States unilaterally to act upon this assumption. This legal difficulty could be avoided if there were an advance agreement upon the point, just as the members of the League are probably now protected by the provisions of the Covenant against any claims of other parties to the Covenant.

It is believed that if some agreement could be reached upon American neutral rights in these situations, the United States might be willing to accept such agreement as a *quid pro quo* for the two points in the Davis declaration, namely, consultation and waiver of neutral rights in case of unanimous agreement.

In view of these facts, it would seem desirable and feasible for the members of the League to convene, in conjunction with the United States, a conference for the elaboration of a convention dealing with the subject of neutrality and neutral rights. The experiences of some three hundred years suggests that any attempt to proceed along the traditional lines followed at the London Naval Conference of 1909 would be productive of no satisfactory results. The crucial point is the definition of contraband. The experience of the World War and of all prior wars indicates the difficulty of reaching any lasting agreement on this point. Certain possible alternatives may be suggested.

Mr. Charles Warren, who, as Assistant Attorney General of the United States during the World War, was charged with the enforcement of American neutrality laws, has advanced certain proposals.[19] One of Mr. Warren's suggestions is that agreement should be reached upon the principle that contraband goods should not be subject to confiscation but that a belligerent would be permitted to requisition any captured neutral cargo, paying the price which the cargo would have brought at its destination. This proposal is an adaptation of the doctrine of "preëmption" which has been practiced from time to time since the seventeenth century. A notable example of its use is found in the practice of Great Britain during the French Revolutionary and Napoleonic Wars. Such a policy has been adopted in the past as a concession to neutrals and for the purpose of meeting objections against the extension of contraband lists. Mr. Warren

[19] See *Foreign Affairs*, XII, 377-94 April, 1934, and *Proceedings of the Academy of Political Science*, XVI, 61-70, January 1935.

has made an estimate of the probable cost to belligerents of such a policy of requisition or preëmption and the cost does not appear to be excessive when considered in relation to general war expenditures. The difficulty with such a plan is, that when one power has command of the sea such an adjustment does not give satisfaction to the opposing belligerent and such opposing belligerent would probably continue to seek to intercept and destroy neutral cargoes bound for the ports of the dominant sea power.

Mr. Warren suggests as an alternative, that the United States (or any other neutral) should embargo the shipment of any goods which either belligerent listed as contraband of war. As a further alternative, the United States might establish an export quota "equal to the amount of such articles which the United States exported to each belligerent during an average of five normal pre-war years."

"The benefit of such a policy would be," Mr. Warren says, "that it would directly penalize expansion of contraband lists. For, any article added to its contraband list by a belligerent would be at once placed on the quota list by the United States, and its export not only to neutral countries but to the belligerents themselves would be restricted to a pre-war export amount. If a belligerent nation considered that any article was of sufficient war-aid to its enemy to be placed on its contraband list, it would find that the United States would equally consider such article of war-aid to *both* belligerents and would restrict its export to both. Thus, for instance, if England should place copper on her contraband list, exports of copper from the United States to England would only be permitted to the extent of the normal shipment to England in pre-war years; and similarly exports of copper to England's enemy and to the neutral countries would be so limited to their pre-war normal in amounts." [20]

Yet this suggestion, ingenious as it is, is faced with a grave difficulty. If the scheme is tested against the situation existing during the World War, it seems obvious that the tendency of the Allies would have been to narrow their contraband lists in order to receive unlimited exports from the United States. On the other hand, the Central Powers, being unable in any case to obtain the shipments, would have been inclined to extend the contraband lists in order to force the United States to establish export quotas and thus to restrict the shipments to the Allies.

Historically, the principal difficulties arising between neutrals and belligerents result from belligerent interference with neutral commerce at sea. This is the problem which must be directly attacked. During the World War the Allies entered into arrangements with private or semi-private organizations in various neutral countries whereby exportations were governed by agreements that the goods would not be reëxported to the Central Powers. Shipments coming within the scope of these agreements were covered by certificates of Allied officials and these certificates sufficed to pass the ships when visited by Allied warships. In the seventeenth and eighteenth centuries, attempts were made to secure free passage by means of certificates issued by neutral officials but this device was unsatisfactory because the belligerents lost confidence in the honesty of neutral certification. Joint certification by both belligerents and neutrals would tend to obviate this difficulty.

In itself, such certification would be insufficient. In the past, neutrals have been accustomed to insist not only on the continuance of their normal peace-time trade but

[20] *Proceedings of the Academy of Political Science*, XVI, 68, January, 1935.

WHAT WILL THE UNITED STATES DO? 141

upon sharing in the abnormally increased trade with belligerents, brought about by war conditions. If neutrals would yield insistence upon this war-boom trade, belligerents might agree on a workable plan to permit uninterrupted traffic between the neutrals themselves. Such a plan would involve total embargoes upon trade with all belligerents. While such a plan might possibly be acceptable to the United States, it would involve grave risks for small powers near the scene of hostilities. Such states might be subject to attack by an aggressive belligerent in case they possessed resources urgently needed by the belligerent and yet not available to it through normal trade channels. The probability that such a plan would lead to the continuous accumulation of war stocks, thus hindering disarmament, may also be noted.[21]

Any general convention on neutrality, concluded in time of peace, should provide for the "solidary attitude" of neutrals as contemplated in the Argentine Anti-War Pact. That treaty does not contemplate an "armed neutrality"; intervention in the conflict is expressly precluded. But a united front, especially in matters of trade and finance, would greatly enhance the likelihood that neutrals would be able to induce the belligerents to respect their treaty rights.

It should be noted that the Senate of the United States has so far indicated its unwillingness to approve the imposition of unilateral embargoes based upon presidential determination of an aggressor. In the winter of 1927-28 discriminatory embargo resolutions were introduced by Senator Capper and Representatives Burton, Fish and others, but no action was taken upon them." [22] In 1933 a resolution authorizing the President, in his discretion,

[21] Cf. C. C. Hyde, "The Arms Traffic from the Standpoint of International Law", *Proceedings of the Academy of Political Science,* XVI.
[22] See Joseph P. Chamberlain, "The Embargo Resolutions and Neutrality," *International Conciliation* No. 251, June, 1929.

to lay a discriminatory embargo on shipment of arms to one of the belligerents passed the House of Representatives but was dropped after the Senate amended it to make the embargo apply impartially to all belligerents. Since 1912 the President has had authority to place embargoes on the shipments of arms and ammunition to the republics of Latin America whenever he should determine that a state of civil war or revolution existed in such countries. The President has frequently exercised this authority. In 1922 the authority was extended to embrace China. When, in May, 1934, the League sought to secure embargoes on the shipments of arms and munitions to Paraguay and Bolivia, the United States took the lead in putting such an embargo into effect. The embargo applied equally to both belligerents. On January 16, 1935, the League decided that Paraguay was continuing to wage war in violation of its obligations under the Covenant and thereafter the embargo remained applicable to Paraguay only. Without further authorization from Congress—which probably could not be obtained—the President of the United States does not have the power to support this action by raising the embargo against Bolivia. Due to geographic and other factors, the inability of the United States to coöperate in this instance will probably not prove to be of great importance. In the case of a war between great powers and involving naval operations, the non-coöperation of the United States might be considered a serious interference with League activities.

However, the imposition of sanctions by members of the League would not be greatly hampered if the United States imposed embargoes on both belligerents. In such a case, all trade by American nationals with either belligerent would be illegal under American law and presumably the United States government would not be

inclined to protect those of its nationals who might seek
to trade in defiance of the prohibition. No help therefore would flow from the United States to the aggressor.
While the United States would also not allow the inno-
cent belligerent to purchase or borrow in its markets, this
deficiency could be supplied by the exporters and bankers
of the sanction-applying states. The United States then
would be sacrificing to commercial rivals, a very lucrative
trade. American exporters would not fail to stress this
feature in an endeavor to have the embargoes lifted. If
the maintenance of the embargoes would contribute to
keeping the United States out of the war, the price would
not be too high.

In the imposition and maintenance of such embargoes,
attention would have to be paid to the old problem of
continuous voyage or ultimate destination. If the
United States would earnestly seek to avoid becoming
embroiled, it would have to face the difficulty by restricting shipments to other countries. The aggressor state,
if a naval power, would certainly not allow the United
States to evade the consequences of its embargo policy
by shipping to the sanction-applying states goods which
could be reëxported to the aggressor's enemy. Perhaps
the difficulty would be insuperable because of domestic
political opposition to so great a loss of American trade
as would be occasioned by further extension of the embargoes. Those nationalistic elements of the population
which now deny the importance of foreign trade, would
be among the first to cry out against an abandonment
of lucrative neutral rights. Perhaps agreement could be
reached in advance covering such a situation, by permitting the United States to use a quota or rationing system
with guarantees against reëxport. It would be necessary
to have clear agreement in time of peace on such a principle if one would avoid the application of the doctrine

of the British Prize Courts during the World War, under which cargoes *en route* from one neutral to another were declared confiscable if it could be argued that the consumption of those goods in the neutral country of destination would release other goods for shipment to the enemy.[23]

If the United States refused to place an embargo on shipments to either belligerent, the conflict with the sanction-applying states would be obvious. It should be repeated that we are here considering cases wherein the United States is unwilling to discriminate against one of the belligerents.

Nothing is clearer than the fact that these problems should be faced and settled in some way before the time of crisis arises. Once war breaks out, agreement will be practically impossible.

Consultation

Regardless of any new consultative pact which might be concluded, the present commitments of the United States are sufficient to make it reasonably certain that it will not refuse to consult with other states, through League channels or otherwise, when an international crisis again arises, provided such crisis seems to have some immediate interest for the United States. It is not to be expected that the United States would immediately consult on such a question as the recent controversy between Yugoslavia and Hungary relative to the latter state's responsibility for the assassination of King Alexander. It is by no means impossible that there should develop more efficient means of consultation on such a question as the war in the Chaco. The advantage of specific treaty provisions lies in the creation of definite

[23] See *The Bonna*, L.R. [1918], P. 123.

procedures. A disadvantage of proposing such a treaty lies in its possible rejection by the Senate of the United States, since such rejection might deter the President from continuing a policy of consultation even apart from treaty commitments. The recent vote on the World Court Protocols indicates that the support of party platform approval of consultative pacts is by no means decisive.

Senatorial approval of consultation, within well-defined limits, may be deduced from the approval of the Argentine Anti-War Pact and from the Joint Resolution of Congress of May 28, 1934.[23a] This was the resolution which authorized the President to impose an arms embargo on Bolivia and Paraguay, "if . . . *after consultation* with the governments of other American Republics and with their coöperation, as well as that of such other governments as he may deem necessary," he found that such action "may contribute to the reëstablishment of peace." [24] Regardless of treaty commitments, the Congress might again pass a similar resolution should the occasion arise.

A general treaty obligation like that expressed in the Four-Power Pact, or implied in the Briand-Kellogg Pact, might give some added assurance to other governments but probably would not greatly affect the actual practice of the United States government. If such assurance is desired, a unilateral declaration of American policy, as suggested by Mr. Davis, might be adequate. There can be no doubt of the President's power to make such a declaration or to act upon it.

It may be suggested also that the present peace machinery of the world is defective in that it fails to afford a means for immediate investigation of factual situations. The League has frequently appointed investigating com-

[23a] Yet deduction is a logical process and therefore not really suitable in estimating the future action of a political body.
[24] Italics are the author's. *Congressional Record,* LXXVIII, pt. 9, 9432.

missions, such as the Lytton Commission. The Japanese attack on Mukden occurred on September 18, 1931. It was not until December 10 that the Council adopted a resolution calling for the appointment of such a commission. It was not until January 14, 1932, that the personnel of the commission was finally approved and the commission did not reach Japan until February 29. In the Shanghai affair, on the other hand, the League acted with great rapidity. The serious fighting began on January 28, 1932. Two days later the Secretary-General of the League proposed that a committee composed of official representatives of the states, members of the Council of the League, should be formed to report on the situation. The United States was asked to coöperate and it did so without, however, permitting its Consul-General to become an actual member of the committee which began to function almost immediately.[25]

In the Greco-Bulgarian frontier incident of 1925, the Council appointed a commission of investigation seven days after the first outbreak. The report came before the Council about five weeks later. In the recent frontier dispute between Abyssinia and Italy, which apparently turned largely on controverted questions of fact, no investigating commission was appointed.

Further detailed analysis of the precedents seems to be unnecessary. Within the present frame-work of the League, improvement is possible. The Permanent Advisory Commission for Military, Naval and Air Questions of the League Council earnestly called attention to the problem in its report on the draft regulations for the execution of Article 4 of the General Convention to improve the Means of preventing War. This report said:

The Commission expresses the opinion that it is essential that the experts who are to serve on the commissions of inspection

25 See Cooper, *op. cit.* 246.

should be appointed as quickly as possible when their services are required. The Commission was unanimous on this point. I am sure all my colleagues will agree with me in holding that the Commission's anxieties are perfectly justified, and in expressing the firm conviction that Governments will at all times be willing to sanction with the utmost despatch the appointment of one of their nationals as Commissioner.[26]

If a plan for permanent investigating commissions could be drawn up, the United States might be able to coöperate, provided such commissions were not made to appear as purely League bodies. The American government has shown a willingness to agree to the appointment of a Permanent Disarmament Commission with broad powers of investigation regarding observance of conventions on disarmament and traffic in arms. It has entrusted broad powers of inquiry to commissions of conciliation set up under bipartite and multipartite treaties. It would seem feasible to include in a general consultative pact, a provision for permanent investigating commissions. The regulations recommended by the League Council's committee for the execution of Article 4 of the General Convention to improve the Means of preventing War, do not meet the needs which have just been suggested. Those regulations look merely to expediting the Council's procedure for appointing *ad hoc* "commissions of inspection."[27]

[26] League of Nations, *Official Journal*, July, 1932, 1200.
[27] *Ibid.*, 1315.

CHAPTER FIVE

CONCLUSION

The "stabilization of peace" is not synonymous with "freezing the *status quo*." International relations are not static. Existing conditions and situations are not perfect. Possibilities of peaceful change are essential to collective security. That logic which traditionally characterizes French thought, demands an alternative means of obtaining security before France will abandon reliance on arms. Peoples and governments which are convinced of the righteousness of their demands for a change in conditions, will not abandon ultimate resort to the sword, unless they are convinced that the pen will be an effective instrument of reason. The shadows of the World War still adumbrate the next war.

The United States sat at the Versailles council table to arrange the post-war settlements. Would it again meet in consultation to revise that settlement? It is most unlikely. The United States is not yet prepared to play a full rôle in world affairs. It is useless here to weigh praise or blame. It is equally useless to ignore the fact. There is much that Europe could do to make more smooth the path of peace without reference to the action or inaction of the United States. The solutions of problems of minorities, of *terrae irridentae,* of the size of land forces and the rearmament of Germany, of spheres of influence in Africa—these and many others do not wait upon the United States. But tariffs, foreign exchanges, and all barriers to trade; naval armaments and the whole political problem of the Pacific and Far East—these and many other subjects are within the realm of vital American interest and probable American action.

It is impossible, but if possible, futile, to lay the blame for the disorganization of peace at the door of any one government; all national houses are made of glass, equally shatterable by the accusing stone. It is more pertinent to ask, what may be done? In this volume an attempt is made to indicate what the United States may contribute to collective security. The United States is not on the defensive. Its policies, like the polices of other governments, are based on enlightened self-interest. As much as any other government, it will make sacrifices for peace commensurate with its appreciation of the dangers which may thus be avoided.[1] If governments be thought of in terms of individual statesmen, it will often be found that those persons are willing to move much faster and much further than their legislative bodies and masses of less well-informed citizens will permit them to move. In other instances, it will be found that they hold back against the pressure of liberal opinion at home.

A theory of "splendid isolation" has long dominated American thought. An appreciation of international interest and solidarity grows but slowly. There are few countries in which there exists a more deeply rooted and sincere popular antipathy to war. When the people of the United States are convinced that a particular policy will substantially contribute to the stabilization of peace, that policy will sooner or later be followed. Like the peoples of other countries, however, Americans are quick to resent the suggestion that they alone should make sacrifices to the cause of peace. They are not now convinced that other nations are prepared to make sacrifices comparable to some which they themselves have been asked to make.

In Europe, certain aspects of foreign policy are

[1] Cf. the statement of Sir John Simon in his radio broadcast of January 3, 1935, relative to the Franco-British conversations and the suggestion for a defensive entente of European air-powers: "We naturally ask what the advantage would be for us and what would be the burden which we would be undertaking." *New York Times,* February 4, 1935.

accepted by the people of the various states as permanent or long-term propositions. Treaties which fall in line with such policies are readily concluded. In the United States, no comparable tradition exists, and each new treaty proposal is viewed with suspicion.

Certain contributions in treaty form the United States has now made or stands ready to make, and these may be recapitulated:

> Conclusion of disarmament conventions applicable to land, air and sea forces.
>
> Conclusion of a convention to regulate and limit the traffic in arms.
>
> Conclusion of some general agreement regarding neutral rights and duties.

Contingent upon the conclusion of a disarmament convention or other general contribution to the stabilization of peace:

> Conclusion of a general non-aggression pact, embodying the pledge to move no armed forces across the frontier. Such a pact must not contain provisions for sanctions or other action to be taken except upon decisions reached independently by the United States at the time.
>
> Conclusion of a consultative pact which contains no advance commitment regarding the actions to be taken as a result of consultation. Such a treaty might contain detailed provisions for procedures of investigation and conference.
>
> Inclusion in a pact of consultation or non-aggression of the non-recognition doctrine and an undertaking to withhold protection from American citizens aiding an aggressor, if the United States independently concurs in identifying such aggressor.
>
> Continuation of the practice of concluding arbitra-

tion and conciliation treaties which do not provide for compulsory reference and which leave the parties free to accept or reject the recommendations of commissions of inquiry or conciliation.

With the limitations indicated, there seems to be no insurmountable obstacle to concluding a general peace pact which would embody all of these provisions. Such merging and consolidation would be in line with recent League practice as exemplified by the General Act for the Pacific Settlement of International Disputes of 1928, and the General Convention to strengthen the Means of preventing War of 1930. There might be real utility in thus universalizing such obligations, and this step would not interfere with the acceptance of greater obligations by those governments willing to accept them.

For the sake of emphasis, it may be desirable also to recapitulate the obligations which the United States is not now ready to assume:

It will not pledge itself in advance to use its forces for the purpose of applying sanctions or enforcing treaty obligations.

It will not pledge itself to entrust to any international body the final decision regarding a breach of obligations or the coming into existence of any duty to act in any way. An exception may be noted in regard to the possible establishment of a Permanent Disarmament Commission and in respect of the International Labor Organization.

It will not wholly abandon its claims to the rights of neutrality, although it will seek agreement upon these rights and their application.

Even in the absence of additional treaties on these various subjects, the United States will probably continue to consult on occasion when it believes its interests will be furthered by such action. It may impose embargoes on shipments of arms and munitions to both belligerents in case war breaks out. It will probably insist upon observing its duties under the law of neutrality and may assume additional obligations within the scope of that law. It will also insist upon protecting its neutral rights with the possible exceptions already noted. It is quite possible that some assurance of such action being taken might be given in the form of unilateral declarations of policy. It can not be said that this is a wholly negative attitude. The United States is indeed ready to make substantial contributions to the stabilization of peace. Domestic difficulties make it impossible for the government to consider going further. International difficulties—particularly in relation to disarmament—have so far made it impossible for the government to go as far as it is willing to go.

If the other governments of the world believe that peace could be further stabilized by the acceptance of existing American offers, express or implied, the road is open and they may take the initiative.

INDEX